McLUHAN AND BAUDRILLARD

"*McLuhan and Baudrillard* is a supremely confident handling of the emergence of McLuhanism in its French context. Genosko has just the right kind of expertise to bring this off, and he does it. This crisply written text is astute and perceptive, with a fine grasp of the central issues, and will appeal to undergraduates and postgraduates across a wide spectrum of disciplines."

Mike Gane, *Loughborough University*

Marshall McLuhan, the media guru of the 1960s, has not been forgotten. Almost two decades after his death, a McLuhan renaissance is under way, fuelled by the very developments in new media technologies he long ago predicted. His famous buzzphrases, "the medium is the message" and "the Global Village," are once again in circulation. Setting out the theoretical and historical context of this renaissance, *McLuhan and Baudrillard: The Masters of Implosion* traces the impact of McLuhan's ideas on French cultural life and in postmodern theory.

Tracing parallels between the so-called "McLuhan Cult" of the 1960s and the "Baudrillard Scene" of the 1980s, Gary Genosko explores how McLuhan's ideas persist and are distorted through Baudrillard's work, via concepts such as semiurgy, participation, reversibility, the primitive/tribal and implosion. He argues that it is through Baudrillard's influence that McLuhanism has had its greatest impact on contemporary cultural thought and practice.

Gary Genosko is Senior Research Fellow of the McLuhan Program in Culture and Technology at the University of Toronto.

McLUHAN AND BAUDRILLARD

The masters of implosion

Gary Genosko

London and New York

First published 1999
by Routledge
11 New Fetter Lane, London EC4P 4EE

Simultaneously published in the USA and Canada
by Routledge
29 West 35th Street, New York, NY 10001

© 1999 Gary Genosko

Typeset in Garamond by Keystroke, Jacaranda Lodge, Wolverhampton
Printed and bound in Great Britain by MPG Books Ltd, Bodmin

British Library Cataloguing in Publication Data
A catalogue record for this book is available from the British Library

Library of Congress Cataloging in Publication Data
Genosko, Gary.
McLuhan and Baudrillard : the masters of implosion / Gary Genosko.
Includes bibliographical references and index.
1. McLuhan, Marshall, 1911– – Influence. 2. France –
Intellectual life – 20th century. 3. Baudrillard, Jean. 4. Mass
media – Philosophy. I. Title.
P85.M23G46   1999
302.23'092'2–dc21   98-48297
CIP

ISBN 0–415–19061–4 (hbk)
ISBN 0–415–19062–2 (pbk)

DEDICATED TO MY FATHER, ERNEST

CONTENTS

ACKNOWLEDGMENTS

Much of the research for this book was supported by a postdoctoral fellowship from the Social Sciences and Humanities Research Council of Canada. This fellowship enabled me to consult the McLuhan Papers in the National Archives in Ottawa, Canada. My old friend Jon Gardiner put me up and put up with me in Ottawa. Derrick de Kerckhove, the director of the McLuhan Program in Culture and Technology at the University of Toronto, provided moral and intellectual support and stimulation, racking his brain for details of events that happened decades ago in response to my obscure questions, and opening his files to me.

I was also provided with the unique opportunity to try out this book in the form of cyber-lectures delivered through the Cyber-Semiotic Institute at the University of Toronto. I would like to thank the master of cyber-ceremonies, Paul Bouissac, and the Institute's designer, Jamieson Cochrane, for their impressive work. Goodbye virtual students, whoever and wherever you are!

I particularly profited from discussions with Mike Gane about the relationship between McLuhan and Baudrillard. Nicholas Zurbrugg helped me publicly air some dirty Canadian linen about contemporary trends in McLuhanism. Richard G. Smith kept me posted about recent developments in the Baudrillard belt of the Midlands, and William Merrin did his best to get me to slow down and give others a chance. Brian Rigby sent me a delightful pamphlet on the French translation of Richard Hoggart containing the wonderful line from Leeds-born poet Tony Harrison: "An Eccles cake's my *petite madeleine*!" Arthur Kroker provided me with his press kit. And JB was amazed that I had written a second book about him, and that it was on McLuhan. Todd Dufresne made sure I didn't forget my psychoanalytic interests. Samir Gandesha and Ben Freedman heard me out on the topics in this book far into many nights. Tanis Kyle and Steve Raizen provided technical assistance.

Hannah, my daughter, and Rachel, my partner, continue to give me the most important kind of support.

I first met Marshall McLuhan in the late 1970s when I was a freshman at the University of Toronto. A few years later, while I was still an undergraduate, the news that the University had decided to close his famous research center so shortly after his death taught me a valuable lesson about academic politics that I have never forgotten.

Since I was a child my father's workshop was filled with televisions of every shape and description. Only the emphasis has changed: working on televisions has given way to thinking about television.

Winnipeg, May 1998

INTRODUCTION

For better and for worse, a McLuhan renaissance is in full swing. Although many of his books are still out of print and his journals[1] such as The *Dew-Line Newsletter* and *Explorations* have acquired rare book status in some quarters, Marshall McLuhan, a thinker of the end of the book, is at home in today's electronic environments where he has been firmly and very much posthumously ensconced; he has even been elevated to the status of, in some instances, a saint. He is, to be precise, a patron saint of *Wired* magazine and a regular virtual sidekick of Camille Paglia. In order to understand why McLuhan is again on the menu, *McLuhan and Baudrillard: The Masters of Implosion* considers the diffusion and lasting effects of his ideas primarily in France and secondarily in Québec.

My first step in understanding McLuhan today is to place him in historical perspective among the francophones. The French reception of McLuhan cannot, of course, be isolated from his international influence in the 1960s and 1970s. Further work needs to done on his influence in Japan, for instance, with special attention given to the debates over the relevance of the "cult of McLuhanism" in the Tokyo press recounted to McLuhan in unpublished correspondence with Kenichi Takemura (*MP* 38/80).[2] From the very outset it needs to be stated that this book does not Frenchify McLuhan but, rather, concerns itself with the McLuhanization of French intellectuals and media workers interested and operating in creative communications and media environments in general. I also owe a debt to the rhetoric, still very much in evidence, of figuring French intellectuals as if they were in some manner equivalent to McLuhan or "French McLuhans."

The debates in French intellectual circles around McLuhan's ideas not only raged widely and intensely during the decades of his greatest influence in the 1960s and 1970s, but the effects of these debates are still being felt today. The McLuhan renaissance is a second coming, of sorts: another quasi-global outpouring of interest and influence tied once again to emerging communications technologies and information systems, and the cunning of capital as it expands into, and transforms for its own ends, these new infrastructures. McLuhanism remains compatible with capital's new means of expansion in

1

the deregulated, post-industrial cyberscape. During the 1980s, McLuhan's work had largely disappeared from view. My investigation of McLuhan's French reception puts this latency period into perspective. The 1980s were also the period of the "Baudrillard Scene," a pop intellectual phenomenon that spread like wildfire through English-speaking countries in the same delirious manner as McLuhan's notions had done earlier in the 1960s and 1970s. For Baudrillard was, for many critics, the postmodern scene *par excellence*.

When I employ the phrase the "Baudrillard Scene," I am denoting the subtitle of the collection of essays, *Seduced and Abandoned*, edited by André Frankovits (1984). In his self-effacing introductory letter, Frankovits makes the astute observation that with Baudrillard's appearance on the Australian academic and art scenes, books by Baudrillard seemed like "after-effects of the circulation of the name." When this scene developed in a Canadian context in the writings of Arthur Kroker and Charles Levin (1984: 13), the scene became a challenge to the "big numbers of the real, power, sex and meaning." "Baudrillard's world," they wrote, "is that of the electronic mass media, and specifically, of television." This world challenges meaning and significance by neutralizing and devalorizing them, leaving only resistance-as-object as a critical political option, what is tagged hyperconformist simulation or giving back to the media the gift of its own cynicism; this came to be identified as both a punk and new wave style. Hence, Baudrillard is thought of as a "French McLuhan." The scene and the challenge both signal the end of the book and the beginning of television; the end of the reading group and the insatiable desire to make the scene.

Revisiting a text such as Raymond Rosenthal's edited collection *McLuhan: Pro & Con* (1968) puts one in a similar scene: the putative end of the book-oriented culture and rise of electronic communications. Book-men will be rendered redundant, for who needs books when we have television? Rosenthal wonders aloud: "What will become of 'us'?" In a proto-Baudrillardian vein, McLuhan beckons everyone into "the act of electronic disintegration," that is, hyperconformity. Rosenthal will have none of this. He believes in critical distance, solitary thinking, and writes against the myths of the McLuhan cult: the big numbers of the real will remain standing; scientific objectivity and practicality will win out; authenticity and resistant artistic genius will prevail; consciousness can survive sensation; and mystical participation needs enlightened individuals. This is all resistance-as-subject. The challenges of both McLuhan and Baudrillard had, in their respective times, to be reckoned with by academics and self-appointed serious thinkers of all persuasions.

Art critics and artists, critical theorists, social philosophers and bluffers of all stripes and disciplines attempted to come to some terms with the phenomenon of the Baudrillard Scene. Like McLuhan's body of work, Baudrillard's writings travel well. Baudrillard came aboard *Artforum* as a contributing editor in 1984–85, in whose pages several translations of his articles appeared. The European art magazine *Flash Art* published critical assessments, as did Canadian art magazines *Parachute* and *Impulse*, echoing the Australian proliferation of translations, interviews and critical articles by the Feral Collective, *Art & Text*, *On the Beach*, etc. By 1984, "simulation" and "hyperreality" had become passwords in the art world. The American publications are too numerous to mention, but the trail was blazed by the Telos group and by Semiotext(e). Baudrillard toured London, New York, Buenos Aires . . . and the small town of Missoula, Montana. Even *The Economist* reviewed *America*. Kroker began to follow Baudrillard around. The American painter Peter Halley thought he could paint hyperreality. Baseball caps emblazoned with "simulacrum" began to appear on the streets of Toronto. Not even sportswear survived the Baudrillard Scene. All the while critical theorists hotly debated whether or not Baudrillard articulated a form of oppositional practice, taking wild swipes at hyperconformist simulation. The term "silent majorities" re-entered the critical lexicon, even if no one seemed to remember the fatal pronouncement of Richard Nixon on November 3, 1969, in his address to the nation on the pursuit of peace in Vietnam, in which he spoke out against the vocal minority who would have America lose the war and bring the troops home: "And so tonight – to you, the great silent majority of my fellow Americans – I ask for your support." The "peace with honor" speech was absorbed into the mass. When 1972 rolled around and ballots were cast and Nixon won the election no one, not even Baudrillard, could measure the effects of this hyperconformity: peace without honor, a nation traumatized, a helicopter hanging over the embassy in Saigon, and Watergate. The masses, as Baudrillard once quipped, prefer media to messages – national psychodramas tailored for the big and little screens.

The writings of Baudrillard represent, then, a vector for the transmission of McLuhan's ideas, often in distorted forms, to be sure. I consider the McLuhan renaissance to be a result of postmodern theory and the enormously influential role played by French social and cultural theory as it has been, and continues to be, translated into English and disseminated across and beyond the disciplines. It is not an effect of an immediate cause. My strategies for understanding the McLuhan renaissance are first to investigate McLuhan's influence on francophone consciousness in general and, second, more specifically, to provide a detailed reading of what every reader of Baudrillard already in some respect knows: Baudrillard's debts to McLuhan are substantial. Further, McLuhan and Baudrillard are the key thinkers to whom postmodernists turn to situate their deviations from them. These strategies provide both historical and theoretical contexts for understanding the significance of Baudrillard for the McLuhan renaissance as a thinker who carried forward and simultaneously spread *macluhanisme*, thus forming, in a way, a bridge between the "McLuhanacy" of the 1960s and 1970s and the renaissance of the 1990s. The Baudrillard Scene contained a good deal of McLunacy. Baudrillard is not, of course, the only vector transmitting *macluhanisme*, but he is the main carrier.

Indeed, the writings of French urbanist Paul Virilio are filled with McLuhanisms, none more evident than a concern with the consequences of the speeding up of communication in its most general sense, which was for McLuhan what enabled implosion to replace explosion as the defining feature of the whirling electric, and soon to become electronic, world.[3] In his remarks on Expo '92 in Seville – which was centered around the theme of the alleged "discovery" of America 500 years earlier and the role played by maritime transportation – Virilio (1992) drew a direct line from the imperial ambition of Caesar to make the world a Roman city to the Global Village of late capital realized through the *agora cathodique* prophesied by McLuhan. My exploration of McLuhan's French reception or, perhaps better, his French revolution, establishes a context for my explicit reflections on the concepts and modes of theorizing shared by McLuhan and Baudrillard, among others.

At the heart of this project is an obvious relationship between the theories and careers of McLuhan and Baudrillard. This relation is obvious in the Barthesean sense of the naturalness of myth in popular culture and wired ideology and, importantly, of media theory itself as it bears on the relation at issue. Andreas Huyssen (1989) sketched this relation in broad strokes in terms of an inquiry into the "hidden referent" of Baudrillard's media-based theory of simulation, a "postmodern recycling of McLuhan" for the 1980s and beyond. The trope of recycling employed by Huyssen is not fully played out in his writing – not everything is recyclable since, after all, only a few key concepts such as the explosion/implosion distinction and the grand, tripartite, periodization of history remain the primary recoverable and convertible materials for Huyssen. Nonetheless, Huyssen's significant contribution highlights the aforementioned issue of the mastery of implosion in the shift from McLuhan's optimism to Baudrillard's cynicism, drawing special attention to the role of media in the theological desires of both thinkers to accede to a postmodern potlatch or a cool, retribalized culture, whose very rhythm would be that of television. Huyssen's intuition is essentially correct, although he provides nothing about the conditions of McLuhan's entry into the consciousness of French intellectuals and cultural *animateurs*.

Although reports of McLuhan's activities began to appear in the French press as early as 1965, he was not well known in French intellectual circles until 1967, the year the first translation of his work, *La galaxie Gutenberg*, was published in Paris and Montréal. *The Gutenberg Galaxy* originally appeared in 1962. In 1966, however, reports of McLuhan's activities in North America began to appear regularly in learned and popular French publications such as *La Quinzaine Littéraire*, *Le Figaro* and *Critique*. The French journalist Naïm Kattan (1965, 1967; also McLuhan 1966), whose location in Montréal gave him access to the places (Toronto and New York) where McLuhan was most active, published widely on his life and work in France and Québec. While it would be an exaggeration to claim that the Cercle Juif de Langue Française in Montréal was a hotbed of McLuhanism, one of its members, Kattan, was very active and wrote to McLuhan on the Cercle's letterhead in November 1965, setting things in motion (*MP* 8–80).

In the momentous year of Expo 1967, an anglophone "intellectual comet" – to use Kattan's imagery – landed in Québec, precisely in the Québec Pavilion, the very site from which McLuhan entered francophone consciousness. It seemed that the Montréal dailies *Le Devoir* and *La Presse* covered every step McLuhan took that month in *la belle province*! The launch of *La galaxie Gutenberg* at the Québec Pavilion on 7 July was a major media event. To be *avec le maître à l'Expo* was a mediatic obsession (n.a. 1967a), whether it was *Sept-Jours*, *Carrefour*, *Science et Vie* or the dailies covering the events. Alain Pontaut (1967a, 1967b) praised Jean Paré's translation while remaining critical of McLuhan's very clever "mosaic method," which was no method at all. Pontaut realized that Expo was a living mosaic of cultures, buildings and tourists that played perfectly into McLuhan's hands, as well as those of his local publisher, Claude Hurtubise. There were critical moments in this coverage already in evidence in 1966 in the separatist journal *Partis Pris* (*MP* 8/85) in which McLuhan, the prophet of the electric age, is not to be confused with his delirious interpretation of electricity, but best "seated on the chair of the age in question!" French Canadian "tribalism" was, after all, as McLuhan himself believed, a consequence of the age of electricity. For McLuhan, Pierre Trudeau, the Canadian Prime Minister of the time, was as tribal as the Beatles.

In France, *L'Express*, *Le Monde*, *L'Aurore* and others followed suit with coverage of McLuhan in 1967; this reporting ranged from the whimsical – overcoming consumer society through *macluhanisme* (Bonnot 1967) – through mild questioning – McLuhan's affirmations are not always convincing (Dommergues 1967) – to full-blown speculation about what should be the proper Gallic response to *la pensée McLuhanienne* (Garric 1967a). In 1968, the virulent responses had been institutionalized to such an extent that one could ask in the pages of *L'Express* why these attacks focussed on McLuhan and not on consumer society (Ferrier 1968–69). By 1970, however, McLuhan had achieved both fame and notoriety among the French intelligentsia, for many of whom he had become an intellectual impostor unable to live up to his initial promises. By the early 1970s, McLuhan was disciplined for university courses in mass communications, after having mesmerized a significant number of sociologists and teachers. Basic works introducing McLuhan's ideas to French students began to appear (Bourdin 1970; Balle 1972). Explication occasionally went against the grain of McLuhan's liberal notion of exploration since his phrase *j'explique rien* was oft-quoted as evidence that he did *and* did not belong in the university. The so-called "revolutionary" aspects of McLuhan's thought were developed by Jean Marabini (1973) through the oft-repeated grouping, sometimes for no more than the purposes of homophony, of Marx–Marcuse–Mao–M(a)cLuhan, and the electronic theology of Pierre Babin found new contexts, applications and audiences for McLuhan's ideas. The radical cell and the church were both perfused with *macluhanisme*.

McLuhan's public profile declined rapidly as the late 1970s arrived, and by 1980 it seemed he could only be read nostalgically. McLuhan's main French translator, Jean Paré, was a well-known teacher in Québec with strong connections with the Hydro-Québec magazine *Forces*, in which his lengthy, favorable interview with McLuhan had been published (McLuhan 1973a). Today, Paré is editor of the mainstream news magazine *L'Actualité*, in whose pages McLuhan's (1980a) prognostications last appeared in 1980, the year of his death. While McLuhan correctly predicted the flood of conservatism and nostalgia that would mark the 1980s, it was not evident that anyone was listening. As he was accustomed to saying, he only predicted things that had already happened, anyway. But the media guru of the 1960s and 1970s has not been forgotten and his ideas remain vital to recent developments in French sociological and cultural theory.

McLuhan's impact in France and Québec was not only deeply felt but came to be regretted in many circles. This phenomenon has not been critically recounted, theorized and scrutinized. I take up these multiple tasks by returning to the popular reports and intellectual debates that accompanied McLuhan's emergence as a fashionable public intellectual, with the goal of reconsidering the key debates of the period. In France as elsewhere, McLuhan was simultaneously a revolutionary, a reactionary, a prophet and an impostor. What, however, do these contradictory figures tell us about the conditions informing the production and legitimation of knowledge in the French context?

In "Before the letter," Chapter 1, I discuss the "obvious" parallels between McLuhan and Roland Barthes that were widely noted by their readers. It is precisely this obviousness that will be interrogated in light of the double tradition of comparing their early writings on popular culture from the 1950s and the attempts to read them together in an entirely unconvincing way as fellow structuralists. In addition to the incorporative gestures that turned McLuhan into a structuralist of sorts, a later development in both the English and French literatures emerged which positioned him as a postmodernist before the letter. In a dizzy logic reminiscent of McLuhan himself, this development implies that he was both a cause and an effect of postmodernism. The rhetoric of associating McLuhan with French intellectuals such as Barthes, Claude Lévi-Strauss and Jacques Derrida was a way of legitimating his work, even if this bringing together of thinkers did not result in detailed analyses of their texts. Besides investigating a range of French affiliations, I want to place the discussion in an international context imbedded in the history of cultural studies. McLuhan, Barthes and Richard Hoggart (read through the lens of his "French reception"), I shall claim, constitute the international cultural studies triumvirate of the 1950s. In the somewhat rarefied specialty area of French cultural studies, it is in the work of Brian Rigby (1994) that one finds detailed consideration of the issues surrounding the French translation of British cultural studies such as those of Hoggart, although no mention is made in his work to the French reception of McLuhan.[4]

In Chapter 2, "The end of the book and the beginning of television," I offer a critical overview of how French intellectuals understood McLuhan's ideas in relation to the question of *écriture* posed by Derrida and others. As the title of this chapter suggests, the post-book age is not that of a general writing but, rather, of television. Indeed, Derrida (1974: 8) ironically pointed out in his essay "The End of the Book and the Beginning of Writing" that the "death of the civilization of the book, of which so much is said . . . manifests itself particularly through a convulsive proliferation of libraries." Whereas Derrida considered this death of the book to be nothing less than the metaphysical exhaustion of full speech, the intimate proximity or presence of voice to thought, the concept and meaning, McLuhan rediscovered the audile universe as the primary space of a tactile electronic culture, and debased writing (the phonetic alphabet, the printing press) as visual and therefore an abstraction from speech concentrated in one sense. Simultaneously, then, McLuhan reaffirms the metaphysics of presence and the secondariness of writing but aligns himself, at the end of book and the beginning of television, with a "grammatology" of sorts based upon his complex sense of a multisensorial acoustic space. Simultaneously, McLuhan's ideas were becoming influential in the formation of communications policy, which I explore through the important role played by Jean Cazeneuve in the dissemination of the master's words through his writings on mass communications and administrative work in a series of influential public posts. In addition, I note several places, for example, in Gilles Deleuze and Félix Guattari's *Anti-Oedipus* (1977), where McLuhan's notions appeared for the sake of the critique of the signifier and the release of flows of language in electric environments.

In "Mac," Chapter 3, I use Jacques Lacan's concept of the *objet petit a* to appreciate the little *a* in the Gallic rendering of M(a)cLuhan's name, not merely in a psychoanalytic sense, but in terms of the genuine intellectual class struggles in Parisian circles that raged around who could claim whom as an intellectual. The Gallic spelling of MacLuhan shows the symbol of lack, originally lacking in the name, that was the cause of the desire of French M(a)cLuhanites. This little something adjacent to the subject, as it were, was a bit of movable type upon which McLuhan himself placed too much emphasis in his history of technological galaxies. Additionally, it needs to be recalled that Lacan conquered the medium of television in a manner worthy of M(a)cLuhan, and that both were thought of as masters of that medium. Incidentally, at least one hermeneut has felt the need to exercise his critical faculties by placing "*sic*" behind the Gallic rendering of MacLuhan as if I were the one engaged in textual acrobatics!

Chapters 4, 5 and 6 all concern the relationship between the writings of Baudrillard and McLuhan. Anyone familiar with the work of Baudrillard, for example, would not fail to be struck by the important influence of McLuhan's ideas on his thinking. A critical understanding of Baudrillard's – among others' – work demands, then, a return to McLuhan in the context of a consideration of the extensions and reworkings of his ideas across the field of

French sociological and cultural writing over the last 30 years. I ease into this approach in Chapter 4 by means of a reflection on the meaning of the term *semiurgy* and similar semiologically inspired neologisms circulated by French intellectuals in the early 1970s, and later capitalized upon by excremental postmodernists such as Kroker in the mid-1980s. Semiurgy is not, I argue against its popular postmodern intellectual definitions, reducible to what McLuhan meant by massage, although the terms are closely related, and even seem to form a kind of retroactively constitutable lineage. My fifth chapter, "More McLuhan than McLuhan," uses the standard Baudrillardian formula of potentialization stated as "more x than x" to describe in general terms Baudrillard's appropriation and distortion of McLuhan's ideas in the context of a detailed commentary upon how concepts such as participation, reversibility, the primitive/tribal, and, importantly, implosion, have passed from hand to hand.

In Chapter 6 I compare McLuhan's and Baudrillard's models of historical phases contained in the theses of *The Gutenberg Galaxy* and *Understanding Media* with Baudrillard's original triphasic model of simulation he developed in *Symbolic Exchange and Death* (1976; trans. 1993). While Baudrillard was, like many others, initially critical of McLuhan's technological reductionism, the vagueness of his central concepts such as hot and cool, and the "implicit finality" of American culture, Baudrillard later adopts some of the worst excesses of McLuhan's sense of historical phases and their blank spots, which I bring into focus in my analysis of McLuhan's comments on the political situation in Québec in the 1970s and the ongoing struggles there against federalism and the politics of language. While it is commonly claimed that McLuhan has made important contributions to what we now refer to as the debate around "globalization," I want to show that his ideas about nationalism and tribalism in particular remain deeply troubling and, if they are "contributions" at all, the time has arrived to review them critically.

Why study French manifestations of *macluhanisme*? Why now? Today, many Canadian intellectuals and cultural workers like myself concerned with information technologies dwell in the shadow of McLuhan, regardless of whether we intentionally seek out the cool shade or are only momentarily escaping the hot sun. Put bluntly: McLuhan is unavoidable. No one would deny that a new generation – mark them with an *x* or any other letter for that matter – is coming of age in the information environment whose emergence McLuhan predicted but did not live to witness. While certain members of an older generation are busily maintaining McLuhan's legacy through personal reminiscences and what they consider to be the long overdue institutional recognition of his accomplishments, especially at the University of Toronto, this new generation is recoding McLuhan's ideas in pop music, alternative theater and across the cybersphere. Claims of misinterpretation are regularly fired from both generations across their respective screens. In between these extremes, in what McLuhan called the resonant interval of tactile interfaces, new contacts and intergenerational connections are being made between academics, artists and businesspersons that shadow things to come and provide more of the same. Unfortunately, when it comes to McLuhan, everything new is old again. It's business, as usual.

To put it somewhat crudely, there are two wildly divergent streams of Canadian work on McLuhan whose leading practitioners are the director of the McLuhan Program in Culture and Technology at the University of Toronto, Derrick de Kerckhove, and at Concordia University in Montréal, the political scientist and performer of theory as fiction, Arthur Kroker. This is the contemporary context in which readers of McLuhan concerned with his French legacy find themselves. Intergenerational struggles around the uses and abuses of the McLuhan legacy go hand in hand with struggles around the profit motive. In one respect, McLuhan is a controlled substance. His work is carefully managed by his literary agent, Matie Molinaro, and his widow, Corinne McLuhan. It was only recently with the publication of *The Essential McLuhan* (1995), a "reader" edited by Eric McLuhan and Frank Zingrone, with a selection of the master's buzzphrases cobbled together by William Kuhns, that McLuhan was collected at all for purposes of undergraduate teaching. This selective re-editing of McLuhan is far removed from a critique of consumerism. Rather, McLuhanism serves as a navigational device that captures the spirit of a wired, cutting-edge youth culture in a business-friendly manner. For what sort of activity is McLuhan a patron saint? The answer is simple: for the electronic counterculture the saint is an oppositional figure and for business a familiar device for the corporate work of colonization. I do not mean to imply, however, that cyberculture is in its whole at odds with corporate interests, a claim that would be ridiculous. Here, then, the broad audiences already recognize the product and on this basis constitute a receptive mass audience. In a 1992 advertisement, Bell Canada promoted its electronic data interchange network (EDI) for business communications with the famous phrase "the m*edi*um is the message": EDI or DIE! Anagrammatic corporate propaganda surfs the new communications technologies.

While "surfing the Net" is a standard buzzphrase employed to diverse ends, it was also a figure that appeared in McLuhan and Quentin Fiore's *The Medium Is the Massage* (1967: 150–51) in the form of a black-and-white photograph of the master on a surfboard, holding onto his hat, as he rode the wave of the electrically configured whirl. One of McLuhan's favorite nautical metaphors – the whirlpool – was taken from Edgar Allan Poe's mariner in the story "The Descent into the Maelstrom." Surfing delivers one from the task of criticism in the same manner as Baudrillard's mode of traveling across the deserts of America in a hermeneutical vehicle figures disappearance as deliverance from critical thought. Recall also that an esthetics of business was the stock in trade of McLuhan as he delivered his fragmented ideas in boardrooms around North America, picking up commissions from ABC (American Broadcasting Corporation) (McLuhan 1971c) to valorize the team concept, dubbed "friendly teamness" in tv news reporting pioneered by ABC, etc. Perhaps Sidney Finkelstein (1968: 122) got it right when he observed that "McLuhan advises the future ruling powers on how to preserve the happy servitude of the new world-wide tribal village."

What I am suggesting is that the McLuhan renaissance is at home in the well-established consonance between postmodernism and late capitalism; in fact, McLuhan's famous phrases function as globally recognizable jingles for the work of multinational trading in digital commodities; yet, the plasticity of McLuhan's thought has and continues to serve just as well as a sign – servitude with a happy face – of resistance to consumer capitalism. This is a contradiction central to the McLuhan legacy. And it is also, as many have pointed out, the double bind of Baudrillard's notion of resistance-as-object. In another respect, then, McLuhan's legacy is controllable in some domains (print) but fundamentally undisciplinable as it escapes into the antipodes of the cybersphere, in which the very notion of control (copyright, the struggles around encryption) is being called into question.

Under the direction of de Kerckhove, a close associate of McLuhan and a secondary translator of his work into French, the McLuhan Program has become an interface of academics, artists and businesspeople all working with interactive new media. The Virtual Reality Artists' Access Program (VRAAP), headed by Graham Smith, provides virtual reality tools such as David Rokeby's Mac-based *Very Nervous System*, which renders sonorous bodily movement. The importance of artist-engineers like Smith and Rokeby was recognized by the Canadian pianist and musical theorist Glenn Gould in 1968, when he heralded the collaborative effort of engineer Walter Carlos and musicologist Benjamin Folkman on the recording *Switched-On Bach* (Gould 1984: 429–34).[5] Just as, today, the Moog synthesizer seems like a relic, in the future contemporary VR technology may also seem like a museum piece. During 1995, de Kerckhove curated several exhibitions on technology and art, one of which was "TechnoArt" at the Ontario Science Centre (OSC) in Toronto. It was organized around the theme of interactivity and called into question the traditional exhibition and its distancing mechanisms. Indeed, the OSC's mandate is to provide a tactile interactive environment. Many of the installations at TechnoArt, including those of Rokeby, Nancy Paterson's ride in the virtual countryside *Bicycle TV*, and Hiroyuki Moriwaki's electric mirror Rayo-Graphy, put the participant's body to work in the virtual environments created by each piece.

VRAAP also has a high-resolution video conferencing system (PictureTel's System 4000) which makes possible virtual seminars bringing together academics and performers across vast spaces and time zones. Taking as a cue Nam June Paik's (1986: 219–22) experiments in what he called "satellite art," such as the New Year's Day 1984 simultaneous broadcast of *Good Morning, Mr. Orwell* from Paris, New York and San Francisco, de Kerckhove has orchestrated several ground-breaking transatlantic contacts. The artistic exploration of interactivity at a distance and the emergence of new spatial sensibilities through the medium of video conferencing has, in the projects with which de Kerckhove has been involved since 1986, exposed by trial and error many bugs and, on occasion, fallen back on faxes, telephones and e-mail. For technical reasons the "trans" doesn't always come off. Transinteractivity is conceived of as a kind of intimacy at a distance, a dialogue of bodies interacting in a virtual tactile space. Many of the performances designed for *Les Transinteractifs*, a transatlantic colloquium in Paris at the Canadian Cultural Center and in Toronto at the OSC in 1988, emphasized telephatic communication: Christian Sevette's *Le toucher transatlantique* would have allowed members of both audiences to bring together two pieces of Michelangelo's *The Creation of Man* in an act of divine inspiration; in *Le baiser transatlantique*, performance artist Orlan proposed to project on a screen the profiles of two persons from each city, turned toward each other, whose lips would meet in a kiss as they continued to speak French and English respectively (de Kerckhove and Sevette 1990: 15ff.). Recently, the McLuhan Program has organized transatlantic and inter-university Canadian video conferences of the more traditional academic sort such as the "World Series on Culture and Technology" between the Program and leading cultural theorists of various host countries, including Baudrillard. These are now a staple of its formidable battery of electronic pedagogical tools. A little more than 15 years after McLuhan's death, the conservative academic community at the University of Toronto finally opened a McLuhan Studies Room in the Faculty of Information Studies. This opening coincided with a preview, by the media giant Southam, of its *Understanding McLuhan* CD-ROM.

Postmodern intellectual entrepreneur Arthur Kroker remains at the forefront of the performance of advanced theoretical speculation. Kroker almost singlehandedly brought McLuhan into postmodern focus – with a Baudrillardian finding device – through his influential journal *The Canadian Journal of Political and Social Theory* (*CJPST*) and in the pages of the provocative books issued by his publishing house New World Perspectives, especially his *Technology and the Canadian Mind: Innis/McLuhan/Grant*, in which he concluded that McLuhan's fate was to be an "intellectual servomechanism" of the technoscape he so brilliantly described (Kroker 1984: 86). The *CJPST* has been superseded by an electronic journal *C Theory*. In the mid-1980s Kroker began issuing supplementary materials such as cassettes (including spoken texts and music such as "Mutant Madonna" and more recently the recombinant experiment in sound called *Spasm*, a CD that features the sounds of virtual reality, that is, processed samples of sound) along with his books, as well as engaging in multimedia performances (Kroker recently completed a European tour in support of the *Data Trash* book with his partner, the designer Marilouise Kroker, and Montréal-based composer Steve Gibson, who provided an ambient soundscape for the spoken performances). The video work of the Krokers includes the *Body Program*, a panicky romp through virtual America, made in collaboration with Stefaan Decostere for Belgium TV. According to Kroker's own promotional materials, he is widely believed to take off from where McLuhan ended in a kind of discipleship in full forward flight.

If the impulse of transinteractivity is the creative interface between the human body and the virtual environment, then Kroker's gesture moves in the opposite direction: the natural body has become obsolete at the hands of new technologies. The so-called panic body – and, more recently, the body in a spasm of contradictory feelings – is defined by the hyper-exteriorization of its organs and viruses and the hyper-interiorization of designer subjectivities (Kroker 1987: iii). Kroker takes McLuhan's thesis of the "outering" of human senses by technology and turns it into an emptying into the technoscape and then a reverse "invasion" of the media environment. Even better, the information highway is paved with human flesh and littered with fresh roadkill run over by the corporate behemoths who are trying to run the road. As catchy as a Kroker buzzphrase can be, he never loses sight of the class struggles being waged over the conditions of access and the social choices implied by new technologies (see Kroker and Weinstein 1994). This point needs to be kept in mind since the McLuhan legacy was singularly devoid of progressive political ideas and remains largely the same today, with a few exceptions. The projects of de Kerckhove and Kroker represent two facets of the Canadian esthetic imagination stirring in the shadow of McLuhan. These two academic outerings in no way tell the whole story of McLuhan today.

The situationist Guy Debord (1990: 33) once wrote of McLuhan that he was "the spectacle's first apologist, who had seemed to be the most convinced imbecile of the century." Debord also noted that even a Global Village idiot like McLuhan eventually realized that mass media cannot deliver on promises of freedom and accessibility. Decades of critiques of McLuhan's techno-optimisim have demonstrated the negative consequences of freedom from fragmentary specialism in un- and under-employment and freedom to be involved in the planetary social process through new technologies requiring high levels of consumption, pay-per-play, and Mcwork in the burgeoning electro-service, server and telecottage industries operating in the ruins of the welfare state. It is important not to lose sight of this critical perspective in today's heady reaffirmation of McLuhanism.

Less an idiot than intellectual jester in the humanist tradition of Erasmus's folly, Joyce's wit, and Rabelais' bawdiness, McLuhan played the clown in order to infiltrate specialist discourses and cross the wires of disciplines and satirize them in a mode he called anti-environmental. While McLuhan may have lacked the sense of folly as a philosophical vocation, by playing the clown he was also playing at being an artist. He chose eclecticism over the effort to synthesize. He used probes, puns, blasts and counterblasts, and the mosaic method instead of integrative strategies. He was a media artist who created the new form that Donald Theall (1971) dubbed the *concrete essay* with its collide-oscopic principles of typographic play, surrealistic juxtaposition of images, and, unfortunately, heavy doses of technological mystification.

All of McLuhan's fooling around had a specific faith underlying it: salvation from the fall of literacy might be found in electric technology (McLuhan 1964: 21), with the proviso that a good deal of suffering (Babel) would be concomitant with the electronic spirit of Pentecost. McLuhan had a deep faith in harmony and wholeness, made manifest by the Holy Spirit of the microchip and a mediatized God, under the unity and governance, not of Rome, but of Bill Gates. Huyssen (1989: 10) brings out McLuhan's media theology quite nicely by asking the reader of *Understanding Media* to perform a thought experiment:

> try an experiment in reading: for electricity substitute the Holy Spirit, for medium read God, and for the global village of the screen understand the planet united under Rome. Rather than offering a media theory McLuhan offers a media theology in its most techno-cratic and reified form. God is the ultimate aim of implosion . . .

It is no wonder that, currently, in the pages of the magazine of which McLuhan is the patron saint, one finds a special issue devoted to "Channeling McLuhan" (*Wired*, January 1996). The three articles by Gary Wolf let McLuhan play the fool but, he is after all "Saint Marshall, Holy Fool." McLuhan's Catholicism is figured in a new age rhetoric of channeling, a televisual notion of wired convergences made possible by new technologies; online, born-again capitalists can "interview" McLuhan by e-mail by channeling a simulation of the saint, a McLuhan-bot, if one cares to play along. The adjectives pile up in an absurd, but entirely familiar, way: McLuhan is a conservative Christian, and an anarchist, to boot; he is not a neo-Luddite, but a mystic. In one respect Wolf has absorbed McLuhan's lessons in *Explorations* from the late 1950s on the liturgical revival to the extent that electronic culture has the power radically to change Christian ritual, demanding "collective liturgical par-ticipation" that is dialogic and creatively passive, in the place of the private reading of the text of the Mass (McLuhan 1957). Getting online is just this kind of ritual.

What is significant about Wolf's emphasis on McLuhan as a "holy fool" is that – and this brings us back to the French reception of McLuhan – this was taken very seriously by some of his French readers such as Pierre Babin (and Iannone 1991) in terms of new Christian approaches to communication. Indeed, it is by posing the question of McLuhan's French reception that an informed approach to the issue of faith may be made that renders moot both Wolf's new agism and Huyssen's thought experiment.

Electronic media frame faith very differently, Babin realized, and he sought to develop, with concepts borrowed from McLuhan, new approaches to communicating faith: "the ear," as he put it, "is the way" of liturgical development, an imaginative, affective and aural framing of faith in what he called the "church of modulation": rock bands, go-go dancers, slide shows, videos, well, anything goes, and once went, too, along with the pews! McLuhan collaborated on a book with Babin in the late 1970s (McLuhan and Babin 1977) and the unpublished correspondence between them (*MP* 18/61) provides a good deal of insight into McLuhan's reflections on the history of the church and the effects of media revolutions on it, from the printing press to the microphone. De Kerckhove (1990), in fact, devotes a chapter of his book *La civilisation vidéo-chrétienne* to the matter of McLuhan's faith in the church, and quotes amply from McLuhan's discussions with Babin. De Kerckhove makes it clear why the ear is the way, citing Matthew 13.9, Mark 4.9 and Luke 8.8, all to the effect that: "Listen, then, if you have ears!" Babin's distinction between the modulation and alphabet churches, the former a warm, resonant space eliciting participation in the multisensorial vibrations, and the latter a clinical space organized for explanation leading directly to understanding, is based on McLuhan's suspicions about the role played by the Gutenberg inheritance in the church. The deleterious effects of the framing of faith are evident in the way in which the catechism is learned, the hierarchical church bureaucracy and, in general, the triumph of the letter, the scriptures and their interpretation, over the spirit, the communication of a living presence. The issue here is not simply the dislodging of the eye by the ear, of seeing by hearing. The danger is that the eye will exclude the ear. The "ear is the way" requires, for McLuhan (quoted in de Kerckhove 1990: 93), a subtle distinction between hearing (*écouter*) and listening (*entendre*); the former requiring visual attentiveness to strings of signs, and the latter adjusting to *la bonne fréquence*, tuning in to the right channel, as it were, or what Babin called modulation, the new style of the electronic church. The church of modulation is making a comeback as a new generation takes charge of moribund youth ministries with a style learned from rock videos and Web sites. Canadian magazines such as *Beyond*, Christian television shows such as FreeTV as well as revitalized youth ministries with a "seeker-friendly" feel are the latest manifestations of McLuhanite Christianity (Sarick 1998). I am not suggesting that this is an improvement over the lugubrious tones of "born again" Christianity, with its conversion fetishism and heavy-handedness that marked the 1980s.

If one stands before a classroom of undergraduates and asks if they are familiar with the name of McLuhan, the answer will undoubtedly depend upon their use of new media technologies. The greater the use, the greater the familiarity. Moreover, the corporate rhetoric of globalization also borrows liberally from McLuhan, and circulates intensely in a variety of media environments and international markets, cluttering our everyday lives. This sort of informal survey is rather ahistorical and, at best, constitutes an inventory of effects *à la* McLuhan himself. In order to avoid a superficial agglomeration of effects, mentions of McLuhan, and sightings of a "McLuhan

Watch," I argue that the McLuhan renaissance may be best understood by reflecting on its French reception, dissemination and transfiguration, plotting its course into the present by means of postmodernism, as well as by following other minor vectorial tributaries. My strategy of critique is both backward- and forward-looking. The question of faith is a case in point, for not only do contemporary reports of a wired Christianity lack historical perspective on McLuhanite Christianity, but the latter's French incarnation in the work of Babin, de Kerckhove and others provides a protentive line forward which has much explanatory, contextual and comparative value regarding this important facet of contemporary McLuhanism.

NOTES

1 Concerning McLuhan's journals, almost no critical attention has been paid to them. I provide the following information as a guideline for researchers. Twenty *McLuhan Dew-Line Newsletters* were published by the Human Development Corporation in New York between 1968 and 1970. The format changed from issue to issue. The designs were adventurous, and several included supplementary materials such as slides and playing cards. It is difficult to find a complete set; not even the University of Toronto Archives holds the complete run. For a brief description of McLuhan's commercialization at the hands of Human Development Corp. President Eugene Schwartz, see P. Marchand, *Marshall McLuhan: The Medium and the Messenger*, Toronto: Random House, 1989, pp. 199–200. Of course, McLuhan was no stranger to promotional activities, a good example of which appeared in a letter he wrote to advice columnist Ann Landers (December 17, 1969) concerning the virtues of the "Dew-Line Deck" (the supplemental playing cards issued with II/3 Nov.–Dec. 1969) as a brainstorming device. Each card contained an aphorism in relation to which problems could be discussed, stormed, bounced off, etc. (see *Letters of Marshall McLuhan*, Toronto: Oxford University Press, 1987, pp. 393–94). The complete run included: I/1 Black Is Not a Color (July 1968); I/2 When You Call Me That, Smile (August 1968); I/3 A Second Way to Read War and Peace in the Global Village (included a Sensory Training Kit consisting of the book mentioned and an exploratory essay) (Sept. 1968); I/4 McLuhan Futuregram, No. 1 (October 1968); I/5 Through the Vanishing Point (November 1968); I/6 Communism: Hard and Soft (December 1968); I/7 Vertical Suburbs and High-Rise Slums (January 1969); I/8 The Mini-State and the Future of Organization (Feb. 1969); I/9 Problems of Communicating with People through Media (March 1969); I/10 Breakdown as Breakthrough (April 1969); I/11 Strike the Set (May 1969); I/12 Ad Verse: Ad Junkt (included slides) (June 1969); II/1 Media and the Structured Society (July–August 1969); II/2 Inflation as Rim-Spin (Sept.–Oct. 1969); II/3 The End of Steel and/or Steal: Corporate Criminality vs. Collective Responsibility (included playing cards) (Nov.–Dec. 1969); II/4 Agnew Agonistes (Jan.–Feb. 1970); II/5 Bridges (Mar.–April 1970); II/6 McLuhan on Russia: An Interview (May–June 1970); III/1 The Genuine Original Imitation Fake (July–Aug. 1970); III/2 The University and the City (Sept.–Oct. 1970).

The other major journal was *Explorations*. The first nine issues are perhaps most widely known since selections from them were published in book form as *Explorations in Commmunication*, edited by Edmund Carpenter and McLuhan (Boston: Beacon, 1960). The first issue of the journal appeared in December 1953, and number nine in 1959. But that was not the end of it. *Explorations* became "a magazine within a magazine" in the University of Toronto alumni association publication, the *Varsity Graduate*. Beginning in the summer of 1964, the *VG* (later *U of T Graduate*) contained an insert of selected articles, edited by McLuhan alone. These unnumbered issues ended with the Christmas issue, 1967. *Explorations* picked up again with issue 21 in March 1968, and this numbered series ended with no. 30 in June 1971. The final two issues appeared in 1972. *Explorations* ceased publication in May 1972. The length of the journal's run (1953–59; 1964–72), in one form or another, is not well known.

2   The McLuhan Papers (*MP*) at the National Library of Canada in Ottawa are an invaluable resource for anyone with a serious research interest in McLuhan's life and work. File 38/80 contains letters from Kenichi Takemura to McLuhan regarding the McLuhan phenomenon in Japan. See especially KT–MM, Jan. 9, 1968 for an overview of McLuhan pro and con in Japanese media.

3   Paul Virilio's debts to McLuhan may be even greater than those of Baudrillard. I make reference to his journalistic report of (1992) "Une exposition très fin de siècle," *Le Monde* (April 16): 26, but this is just the tip of an iceberg. Virilio and McLuhan's key interests include fields or environments of perception, speed and war. Indeed, some of Virilio's central notions, such as the esthetics of disappearance, are carried on a McLuhanesque fusion of medical metaphor (picnoleptic fit or *petit mal*) and measurement (beyond the speed of sound in a relational speed space, the lost dimension). It is instructive to read Virilio's (1989a) *War and Cinema*, Patrick Camiller (trans.), London: Verso, with McLuhan and Fiore's (1968a) *War and Peace in the Global Village*, New York: Bantam. Both concern the creation of new environments by media technologies from which, in turn, further technologies emerge. It is the "trade in dematerialization" in the global environment of weaponry that interests Virilio; that is, the capacities of technologies either to render things visible (by means of radar and thermal imaging) or to render things invisible (stealthy objects). Virilio's thesis that the "history of battle is primarily the history of radically changing fields of perception" leads him to focus on media of all sorts, especially film. The war film need not depict battles since a color stock in itself, for example, has the power to create technological and psychological surprises. American technicolor, as opposed to German Agfa color, agitated Joseph Goebbels, the "patron" of German cinema in World War II, to such a degree that he banned films made with the latter because he thought their quality was shameful. Virilio believes that Francis Ford Coppola's *One from the Heart* is more of a war film than *Apocalypse Now* because the director was consumed by his use of military equipment such as the Xerox "Star" naval computer system. Virilio moves deftly from the cinema, to weaponry, to the pin-up, the bunker and other military architectures, to chronophotographic rifles in a truly McLuhan-like marshaling of anecdotal evidence. Reading Virilio is a bit like taking a stroll through the Musée National des Techniques in Paris, paying special attention to the radio, television and photography sections, and allowing the photographic rifle and sundry apparatuses to shine in all of their

brilliant suggestiveness. Yet what separates Virilio and McLuhan is the latter's criticism of the dominance of the eye. For Virilio the war machine is fundamentally an ocular machine. See John Fekete (1977), "Notes toward a Critique of McLuhan's Polemic against Vision," in *The Critical Twilight*, London: Routledge, pp. 213–15. Incidentally, Fekete was one of the few English critics to ruminate about the McLuhan–Derrida ligature: it was a standard, almost automatic, comparison for French readers. See Fekete's suggestions regarding the general oral form and general writing, "Massage in the Mass Age: Remembering the McLuhan Matrix," *Canadian Journal of Political and Social Theory* 6/3 (1982): 62ff.

4 Brian Rigby is connected with the English journal *French Cultural Studies*. His monograph appeared in (1994) *"Popular Culture" in France and England: The French Translation of Richard Hoggart's "The Uses of Literacy"*, Hull: The University of Hull Press, and it is full of fascinating observations on French translations of Richard Hoggart's seminal book in British cultural studies, (1957) *The Uses of Literacy*, London: Chatto & Windus, which appeared in French in 1970 under the title *La culture du pauvre: Etude sur le style de vie des classes populaires en Angleterre*, Paris: Minuit. The book was translated by Françoise and Jean-Claude Garcias and Jean-Claude Passeron, with an introduction by the latter. Translating Hoggart into French is not simply a matter, as Rigby notes with evident delight, of "making an Eccles cake a madeleine." Rigby's concern with Hoggart parallels my own interest in the French translations of McLuhan.

5 The relationship between Glenn Gould and McLuhan is much more interesting than that implied by my reference to Glenn Gould (1984) "The Record of the Decade," in *The Glenn Gould Reader*, Tim Page (ed.), Toronto: Lester & Orpen Dennys. There are a smattering of references to McLuhan in *The Glenn Gould Reader*. Gould's 1966 essay, "The Prospects of Recording," uses McLuhan's idea that "the content of new situations . . . is typically the preceding situation" to good effect in relation to the ways in which electronic scores have conventional textures superimposed upon them (p. 345). See also Gould's letter to McLuhan, Jan. 24, 1965 in (1992) *Glenn Gould: Selected Letters*, John P. L. Roberts and Ghyslaine Guertin (eds.), Toronto: Oxford University Press, p. 70. The general tone is that McLuhan's concern with media complements Gould's interest in processes of production. I discuss Gould's relation to Deleuze and Guattari at length in my (1998) *Undisciplined Theory*, London: Sage, pp. 73–81.

1

BEFORE THE LETTER

It is commonplace for both French and English critics to mention the relationship between the writings of McLuhan and Barthes in the course of their reflections on popular culture. One could catalog an impressive inventory of reminders of the parallel concerns of *The Mechanical Bride* (McLuhan 1951) and *Mythologies* (Barthes 1957). It needs to be kept in mind, however, that it was the question of McLuhan's relation to the practices of structuralism that often animated such comparative observations, and that Barthes was not always the first figure suggested to French readers of McLuhan. In terms of reading practices, this meant it was the work of Claude Lévi-Strauss that came to mind in the first instance. In 1966, the year McLuhan's writings first received widespread critical exposure in France, the journal founded by Georges Bataille, *Critique*, published a review by Paul Riesman (1966) of the English editions of *The Gutenberg Galaxy* and *Understanding Media*, while Maurice Nadeau's *La Quinzaine Littéraire* carried an interview with McLuhan by their Canadian correspondent Kattan (1966). In addition, by 1966, Barthes had, in fact, begun to turn away from the structural analysis of narrative.

Riesman (1966: 174) thought that traditional social scientists would have difficulty with McLuhan's mosaic method since it was unlike the methodologies with which they were accustomed to working. Moreover, it would be pointless to judge McLuhan's work on the basis of such methodologies since his debt was to literature rather than sociology. For Riesman, McLuhan was more of a novelist sketching the personalities of technologies than a sociologist. Even so, Riesman believed that McLuhan left too much to the reader's imagination in his infatuation with collecting and juxtaposing quotations and ideas. Despite this literary debt, McLuhan is not exempt from the so-called error of thinking that "the simple spatio-temporal juxtaposition of things – pseudo-Einsteinian approach – constitutes a sufficiently powerful analysis of their relations" (Riesman 1966: 174–75). If social science errs on Newtonian rather than quantum grounds in the pursuit of rigor and exactitude, McLuhan stretches the limits and coherence of "social Einsteinism" as a critical approach relevant to understanding social change. What is interesting about this criticism is that McLuhan's method is thought to suffer from the very thing that would win it praise a few years later in some Anglo-American circles. Riesman's critical discussion of the mosaic method itself roams freely across the disciplines. He refers to it in psychoanalytic terms as "a chain of free associations" and treats it as a biological entity whose parts, like the amputated limbs of certain organisms, may engender new organisms since the part contains details of the whole.

Riesman situates McLuhan in relation to two key French figures. Like Jacques Ellul, McLuhan takes critical notice of the mechanization and de-humanization of persons and the disappearance of individualism since the Renaissance. While Ellul bases his social criticism and vision of the future on the extension of his general concept of technique, McLuhan considers media of communication to be vehicles of radical change, and this change will be marked by the re-emergence of a healthy and wholesome tribalism. The second figure to whom Riesman refers is Lévi-Strauss. The analyses found in *Understanding Media* are in agreement with the "spirit of the times," Riesman thinks, despite the unverifiability of the hypotheses advanced in this book. The insight into "the inherent message of the structure of the media of our age" suggests to Riesman (1966: 179) that the point of attack of McLuhan and Lévi-Strauss is "formally the same," even though their goals and methods are different. McLuhan and Lévi-Strauss do not meet by chance for

> these two researchers have recognised independently of one another that the structure of communication also contains a message and it is often the message which is the most important. But for Lévi-Strauss the importance of this message [i.e., rules of kinship and marriage assure the exchange of women between groups, just as linguistic rules assure the communication of messages] is that it reveals at the level of the unconscious the structure of the human mind while, for McLuhan, this message has a certain effect on the mind of man without him being aware of it.
>
> (Riesman 1966: 179)

It is in light of this difference that Riesman criticizes McLuhan on the ground that he has an inadequate concept of the nature of man and cannot explain whether or not his "man" receives the messages inherent to the structure of the media. McLuhan recognizes this problem without solving it, turning instead to the observation, for instance, that it is not easy to explain the fact that the transformative power of the media can be ignored by so many.

In Riesman's staging of an early encounter between McLuhan and structuralism, McLuhan proves to be an unworthy partner for Lévi-Strauss. Read retrospectively, this was a sign of things to come, since McLuhan's French and English readers would struggle to find a mode of analysis into which he would fit with a minimum of theoretical violence. The terms of

McLuhan's relationship to structuralism would be drafted again and again without, I want to show, much success. It is in this context that Barthes would emerge as a fellow traveler whose path through literature to the social paralleled that of McLuhan and whose relationship to structuralism was troubled enough to allow for flexibility in the comparison. Style supplants method as the common measure of both men.

NOMINATING BARTHES

Writing in the daily newspaper the *Toronto Star* in the summer of 1978, the Canadian journalist Robert Fulford asked his readers to consider the complexities of a recent book by Barthes (*Roland Barthes by Roland Barthes*) under the provocative title of "Meet France's Marshall McLuhan." Aside from the title, Fulford said little concrete about the relationship between McLuhan and Barthes, dwelling instead upon the "impenetrability of [Barthes's] thought" and the perils of an intellectual celebrity who has been canonized for writing against the canon, as it were. Fulford's single reference to McLuhan read:

> Like Marshall McLuhan, [Barthes] sees the way that you express yourself as potentially more important than what you actually say. Barthes sees a great historic drama in the attempts of various underclasses to imitate the style of those who have power.

The Barthesean theme of the weak "stealing Language" from the sites of Power, which he expressed in *Mythologies* (1957) as the ubiquity of bourgeois ideology in French society of the 1950s and the necessity of all other social classes to "borrow" from the bourgeoisie, became for Fulford a way of situating Barthes's own intellectual development and rise to international intellectual fame. This modest newspaper article provides an early example of the rhetoric of the search for the "French McLuhan."

It is not only that McLuhan and Barthes shared an interest in popular culture and the analysis of forms of expression; rather, Fulford implies that the relation between McLuhan and Barthes is based upon the impenetrability of their respective writings. In short, the writings of French intellectuals are just as impenetrable as the work of McLuhan, and equally insightful, if not audacious. "From gurus we always get enigmas," Fulford wrote some years earlier in the *Star* (Sept. 1971), referring to McLuhan among others.

"Meet France's Marshall McLuhan" did not go unnoticed by McLuhan. A few weeks after its publication he wrote a letter "To the Editor of the *Toronto Star*" in response to Fulford. Deepening the connection between himself and Barthes, McLuhan (1987: 539–40) wrote that Barthes "once asked me to collaborate with him on a book." Although McLuhan did not elaborate on his contact with Barthes, he was flattered to be placed by Fulford in the company of Barthes. I shall elaborate on McLuhan's meetings with Barthes and the "myth" of their ill-fated collaborative project later in this chapter. In the meantime, and despite the remarks of the editors of McLuhan's *Letters*, for whom the fact that Fulford did not explicitly refer to McLuhan's work as "impenetrable" provides a posthumous line of defense, McLuhan himself drew the obvious conclusion: "Fulford sees Barthes as impenetrable as myself." McLuhan specifies that the special character of his "impenetrability" results from his study of effects rather than his theorizing; to use other words, he claimed to study patterns without theories. Equally significant, however, was McLuhan's naming of Barthes's work: "As for Barthes, he is a 'phenomenologist' – that is, one who tries to see the patterns in things while also playing along with the dominant theory of his world."

I will use this misidentification of Barthes as the occasion for a reflection on McLuhan's relationship with structuralism. In exploring this relation, two perspectives need to be distinguished. First, some of McLuhan's French readers aligned his work with multidisciplinary structuralist research as it developed through the late 1950s and into the 1960s. McLuhan was either a precursor of structuralism or a fellow traveler. Finding McLuhan a place in a recognizable stream of research was a normalizing and legitimizing gesture, since it provided a ready-made context of understanding for his work, even if this contextualization relied upon a negative criterion such as "impenetrability" to make the connection. The appeal to structuralism as a means of connecting Barthes and McLuhan is even more strained if it is recalled that by the time of the publication of *Roland Barthes par Roland Barthes* (1975), Barthes had abandoned the technical demands of structuralist method and disavowed the orthodoxies of literature for an autobiographical writing in which he treated himself "as an effect of language."

Second, McLuhan's own "understanding" of structuralism and phenomenology resulted from his translation of general orientations in these areas into the interpretive double of figure/ground. On the face of it, Barthes was certainly not a phenomenologist; yet any reader of the essay which grounds theoretically Barthes's little cultural sketches or "mythologies," "Myth, Today" in *Mythologies*, would admit that his description of the bi-planar structure (full of meaning, yet formally empty) of the mythical signifier of the second-order semiological system of mythology is richly phenomenological (the final term of the signifier–signified–sign triumvirate becomes the first term or signifier of the mythical system). Barthes describes how myth gets a hold of first-order linguistic signification for its own purposes. Form plays a game of hide and seek with meaning, holding meaning at a distance and in turn hiding in it; form also preys parasitically upon meaning by emptying it of history, reality and contingency. Indeed, in an earlier book, *Michelet par lui-même* (1954), Barthes had undertaken a phenomenologically inspired description of selected "existential thematics" pertaining to the sensations and substances at work in Michelet's imaginative histories. These observations do not commit one to McLuhan's position, since neither of the "two Barthes" to which critics commonly refer were, strictly speaking, phenomenologists. To use slightly more positive terms, McLuhan's naming of Barthes was not as ridiculous as it first appeared.

CALLING ALL STRUCTURALISTS!

In the late 1960s in Québec, the translator, writer and editor Jean Paré (1968: 9–10) had attempted to identify McLuhan as "an estranged parent" of the structuralists, rather than a precursor or product of structuralism. While Paré developed the figure of McLuhan as an "amateur structuralist," his efforts at establishing his next of kin quickly unraveled with the qualification that McLuhan is not really a structuralist, since he is neither part of this diverse movement nor a disciple of one of its figures or methodological variations. As the figure of McLuhan and structuralism began to lose touch completely, Paré sought a safe common – albeit vague – ground: McLuhan became a contemporary of the practitioners of structuralism. Paré's final figure expressing the relationship between McLuhan and structuralism is of "a circle inside of a polygon" suggesting that the relationship of the former with the latter is tangential, rather than being totally oppositional. This would not be the last feeble attempt to unite McLuhan and structuralism.

Praising structuralism for both its housekeeping skills and ability to mirror mass-mediated confusion, Edward Said (1971: 56–57) set this method in and against the North American sprawl of McLuhanism. Said mentioned nothing, however, about the spread of *macluhanisme* among the francophones. Kroker (1984: 78) referred to McLuhan as "structuralist (before his time)," picking up the pieces of a long series of disjointed efforts to rearrange a marriage that was, from the outset, made somewhere other than in heaven.

During the early 1970s, James M. Curtis addressed the issue of McLuhan's relationship with French structuralism in two articles, the first of which focussed on Lévi-Strauss, and the second on Barthes. Curtis's (1970) hyberbolic importation of McLuhan into his review of *The Languages of Criticism in the Sciences of Man* provides the occasion for the claim – echoing Riesman – that McLuhan and Lévi-Strauss "share almost everything." What Lévi-Strauss and McLuhan share in particular is "an oracular style, a disregard for academic conventions, and a wide public impact, a combination which naturally arouses their more traditional colleagues to a near-apoplectic frenzy" (Curtis 1970: 62). Their relationship is based first and foremost on style, one marked by ambiguity and portentousness. Beyond this issue, Lévi-Strauss and McLuhan are said to share an attitude; their respective writings have had a wide and major impact; they have both been the target of their colleagues' outbursts. Only the matter of style opens the door ever so slightly to a consideration of the relationship between their writings. But since the appeal to style in this instance remains undefined and vague, we should expect little from such textual considerations.

While the "family resemblances" first postulated by Paré dissolved into abstract geometrical lines, Curtis frames his sense of resemblance with the wide borders of a general sociology of knowledge production, in which references are made to the reception of interdisciplinary work in a disciplined academy and the phenomenon of university professors who become popular sages. It follows for Curtis that two innovative thinkers who "share everything" – but may, in fact, have nothing in common – may be said both to practice a certain brand of "structuralism" full of creative play. This structuralism is more poetic than analytical and it entails the implosion of the subject/object distinction, the end of the primacy of empiric evidence, and the collapse of distinct disciplines. These are the main features of the post-Newtonian world of the human sciences. For Curtis, both Lévi-Strauss and McLuhan are in these terms practitioners of "social Einsteinism." These features allow Curtis (1970: 65) to apply to McLuhan's *Understanding Media*, a book he admires for its puns and non-sequential analysis, what Eugenio Donato wrote of Lévi-Strauss's *Le cru et le cuit*: "it is impossible in a work such as [this] to separate myth and literature, science and interpretation, analysis and criticism." Ultimately, Curtis (1970: 67) will posit the convergence of "the linguistic concept of structure, anthropological findings, modern literary criticism, and the interests of McLuhan and others in contemporary society . . . in the study of myth." Taken together with the matter of style, Curtis's emphasis on myth facilitates the inclusion of Barthes in his stable of French structuralists whose work lends itself to somewhat banal comparisons with that of McLuhan.

In his second essay, Curtis is content to rehearse the features of the conceptual universe of "social Einsteinism," but in relation to McLuhan and Barthes. The work of McLuhan and Barthes is, he claims at one point, post-modernist, and the consideration of their work "elicits a better understanding of the postmodernist situation as whole" (Curtis 1972: 143). Here, post-modernist seems to be synonymous with "social Einsteinism." It is not at all evident that one can be both structuralist and postmodernist since the latter has a particularly active component of anti-structuralism. Further, Curtis compares passages in Raymond Picard's *New Criticism or New Fraud?* (1969) and Sidney Finkelstein's *Sense and Non-sense of McLuhan* (1968) as instances of two virulent attacks on Barthes and McLuhan which were provoked by their similar styles of presentation. These venomous responses enable Curtis to hold together McLuhan and Barthes by means of external criteria; here, quite explicitly, in terms of provocations.

Curtis's interest in style is at times strikingly McLuhanesque since he is concerned with the effects of non-sequential writing rather than with analyzing its features. He is content not to face the matter of style squarely but, rather, to sustain McLuhan's resemblance to Barthes on the most general level, since they are both interested in contemporary society, and this interest does not work itself out in Marxian terms (Curtis 1972: 140). This unanalyzed anti-Marxism clears the ground between Barthes and McLuhan so that Curtis may listen to the "echoes" between sentences from Barthes's *Mythologies* and McLuhan's *Understanding Media*. Although these sounds are not discordant, the formal relations between Barthes's cultural sketches and McLuhan's series of exhibits in *The Mechanical Bride* are in agreement. Style is, it seems, nothing more than this kind of agreement. Any reader of these two texts can master style by noting the obvious.

Mass-produced objects such as cars and toys, including certain materials (plastic), as well as performances, exhibitions, films, food and drink, and sporting events, all yield their mythological significations to Barthes. His investigations into myth often commence with representations of events and objects in popular French print media. Women's magazines such as *Elle*, newspapers like *Le Figaro*, and glossy newsmagazines along the lines of *Paris Match* are for Barthes treasure-troves of myths. The Barthesean mythologist may study anything since myth touches and corrupts everything; even those objects that resist myth are "ideal prey." Likewise, McLuhan's commentaries on the folkloric landscapes of everyday objects are inspired by advertisements, the organization of newspapers, comic books, popular magazines (*Reader's Digest*, *Time*, *Life*, *Fortune*), detective novels and various manifestations of the ligature of sex and technology (drum majorette, chorus line, glamor girl, etc.).

But readers of Barthes would be familiar with his early contributions to Marxist scholarship in the pages of the journals *Esprit*, *Combat* and later *Arguments*, on topics as diverse as the theater of Bertolt Brecht and *le nouveau roman*. No reader of *Mythologies* would have overlooked one of the key figures of Barthes's political semiology of myth: inversion. Armed with Marx's image, then, Barthes read the myths of France as it became a consumer society in terms of the processes of bourgeois ideology which gave a universal standing to their particular historical status. The political task of the mythologist was to "upend the mythical message" by revealing how bourgeois ideology "ex-nominates" itself while contaminating every event and object. Ultimately for Barthes, semiology, too, became a myth whose distortions in the name of a science of signs and a science of literature required unmasking. I do not mean to suggest that Barthes's semiology retained the political concerns of *Mythologies*. Although Barthes did not develop a political economy or even sociology of the sign in the manner of Baudrillard, he employed the concept of a "deciding group" that influenced individual use by controlling the language, for instance, of the fashion system. In Barthes's *Elements of Semiology*, first published as an essay in 1964, use is guided by the fabricated languages or "logo-techniques" of the "deciding groups," regardless of whether these groups are narrow and highly trained or diffuse and anonymous. The restriction of speech results from socio-semiotic determinations at the level of the system. This is one of the features of Barthes's semiology that is often overlooked.

The question of style is not so much a matter of the impact of McLuhan's and Barthes's rhetorics as an issue of McLuhan's translation of concepts into his own terms in the absence of an adequate table of conversions. Barthes was always much more explicit in his recycling of concepts, even if he often insisted on redefining them in confusing ways. His unfortunate penchant for the constitutive redefinition of linguistic terms produces an awkward vocabulary in which "arbitrary" means signs formed by the unilateral decision of a deciding group functioning like the superego, one might imagine, behind the parade on the collective catwalk, and "motivated" refers to the analogical relation between signifier and signified. Thus a Barthesean semiological system may be both arbitrary and motivated, a contradiction in linguistics terms, many of which he retains and employs in standard ways. But McLuhan, as Michel Vermillac (1993: 55–56) observes in his unpublished *thèse de doctorat*, did not provide a code that would help his readers decide about the status and relation of the heterogeneous fragments in which he wrote. McLuhan provided no key to the hierarchy among the fragments, and gave little direction about whether a given passage was intentionally insightful, accidental, comic or purely stylistic. The "mosaic method" was characterized, according to Vermillac, by a "generalized indifferentiation" which made McLuhan "neo-baroque" and "postmodernist before the letter." The absence of this code allowed McLuhan to be many things for many people and, more importantly, also enabled him to appear to be mining a number of intellectual veins.

In a letter to anthropologist Edmund Carpenter, McLuhan situated the work of Lévi-Strauss in the Cartesian tradition, which he described as working on figure minus ground (1987: 477). Against this tradition, McLuhan approached phenomena through their grounds, which he sought to feel. In spite of this important difference, McLuhan still referred to his approach as "structuralist," and in the same breath as "existentialist." His explanation, in a letter to Marshall Fiswick written a year later, was twofold: "The reason that I am admired in Paris . . . is that my approach is rightly regarded as 'structuralist'." Moreover, "nobody except myself in the media field has ventured to use the structuralist or 'existentialist' approach" (1987: 506). McLuhan suggested in this letter that *The Mechanical Bride* was in some sense "existentialist." By this term McLuhan suggests that his first book recorded the perceptions of his experience of objects and tried to avoid what he thought of as a moralizing tone, which was a "poor guide" in decoding social myths.

The problem with so-called "phenomenologists" such as Lévi-Strauss, McLuhan believed, was the "left hemisphere tradition" of groundless, pure ideas (*MP* 20/22 McLuhan to C. Brooks, May 16, 1977) in which they worked; moreover, they ignored the study of effects, environments or grounds. McLuhan could take the name "structuralist" since his focus subsumed this approach without succumbing to its overemphasis on abstract forms. A clarification is in order. It may be, as Curtis suggests, that the "medium is the message" entails the study of *langue* rather than *parole*. McLuhan approached figure through ground in order to understand their interplay or Gestalt. The medium may be the figure of the message's ground, or vice versa. This makes McLuhan's "structuralism" Barthesean to the degree that Barthes's particular brand of semiology taught a related lesson with regard to the *langue/parole* distinction. Barthes's semiological extension of the linguistic distinction between *langue* and *parole* led him to reflect upon the "reciprocal compre-hensiveness" of the terms in the dialectic of social object and individual act. Barthes was interested in the semiological prospects of such a distinction, and they were for him brightest in the case of the garment system, as he would show in detail with regard to the written systems of fashion in *Système de la mode* (1967). McLuhan's interest in figure/ground interplay allowed him to take many labels since his work was neither trapped in the study of pure form nor merely a registry of disconnected effects. His "inventories of effects" such as *The Medium Is the Massage* (with Fiore 1967) and *War and Peace in the Global Village* (with Fiore 1968a) did not appear until the late 1960s and were marked by his interest in environments, that is, total containers which recode sensory life.

McLuhan was not well read in structuralism. His reading of Jean-Marie Benoist's *The Structural Revolution* in the late 1970s, however, conjured for him the image of the x-ray characteristics of the electric age, one of whose effects he believed was the structural method itself, with its abstract, disembodied patterns.[1] McLuhan's terms of translation had by then changed, even though he continued to refer to structuralism as phenomenology, while thinking of phenomenological philosophers such as Jean-Paul Sartre in terms of their supposed responses to the violent, discarnate x-ray favored by structuralism. "Phenomenology" – that is, structuralism – in McLuhan's words was, echoing the language he developed in *The Gutenberg Galaxy* (1962: 107ff.), "light-through" and therefore a televisual pattern through which light travels (a kind of x-ray), as opposed to "light on," with which he associated visual intensity, a blinding bias for fixity (of point of view) and literal interpretation. McLuhan's approach to the history of French philosophy was novel, indeed, for he read the Cartesian tradition in terms of the effects of electricity.

My goal here is not to explain away McLuhan's misuses of terms. His handling of methodological labels was so obviously misleading that merely to repeat this would be uninteresting. There is little point in "correcting" such glaring misnomers as McLuhan's (1987: 528) reference to the practices of Yale Derrideans as "phenomenology as it is currently in vogue at Yale and elsewhere." McLuhan's penchant for the translation of concepts into his own loosely defined nomenclature, making available only vague tables of con-version, might be called Barthesean in scope and intensity. While it is well known that Barthes did not honor the concepts he frequently borrowed from several disciplines, he normally provided a table of conversions.

ST. LOUIS/PARIS/BIRMINGHAM

In the study of popular culture in the 1950s, *Mythologies* had an important precursor in McLuhan's *The Mechanical Bride*. For while, as Vermillac puts it, "this *Fiancée* recalls to our French ears certain pages of *Mythologies*" (1993: 30), McLuhan's political position in this book was on the face of it distant from that of Barthes. Despite this distance, there were points of contact and numerous devices used to establish it. Vermillac suggests that "McLuhan mentions as one of his fondest memories the fact of having shaken hands with Roland Barthes, a thinker for whom he had great respect" (1993: 30). Whatever the origin of this "memory," suffice to say that McLuhan's sense of mythology was not explicitly Barthesean, even though it did not completely eschew politics. The meetings of McLuhan and Barthes still endure as myths; whether they took place on paper or in a café seems a moot point, but one worth pursuing nonetheless.

In the "Preface" to *The Mechanical Bride*, McLuhan reveals that he will "cooperate" with the whirlpool action of the "new commercial education" of the mass media. He does not use the figure of inversion. Rather, McLuhan "reverses" the direction of advertising, turning it against itself, forcing it to enlighten as opposed to devouring its "prey." McLuhan situates the target audience, at first figured as "prey," at the center of the mediatic maelstrom. This vantage point enables one better to witness and analyze the action at hand. And from this critical observation "it is hoped," McLuhan adds, "many individual strategies may suggest themselves" (1951: v). The lesson McLuhan learned from Poe is well known: if one struggles against the current of a whirlpool, one will drown; if, on the contrary, one observes and rides the current, waiting for an opportune moment to save oneself by breaking out of it, then one is likely to survive. "Cooperation" is a key but not the only important factor, since hope hangs between capitulation and the formation of a personal strategy that is not necessarily oppositional. Between a paralyzed and an energized mind there is for McLuhan the privileged attitude of amused and rational detachment, of watching oneself sink in order to swim. This attitude was McLuhan's remedy for the ills of passivity produced by mechanization and homogenization. "The reader has to be a second Ulysses in order to stand the siren onslaught," as he put it, shifting from Poe to Homeric myth in the process (1951: 97), but without abandoning the nautical metaphors he favored.

McLuhan was not prevented from identifying an attitude at work in advertising which did not want to be named. Just as Barthes argued that the bourgeoisie "ex-nominates" itself, obliterating its name so as to become the unnamed source of meaning, McLuhan explained in similar terms in "The Ballet Luce" in the *Bride* that the style and technique of *Time* magazine "constitute a most influential set of attitudes which are effective precisely because they are not obviously attached to any explicit doctrines or opinions" (1951: 10). McLuhan sensed the process of "ex-nomination" in the way a magazine provides its readership with certain attitudes, emotions and signs of their difference from other audiences, building coherence through, in the case of *Time*, a kind of formulaic diary writing. Depoliticized speech has political effects, McLuhan observed, even though he did not investigate them beyond noting the mindlessness and infantilism of *Time*'s readers and expressing the fear that one day a "goose-stepping reader" might make a grab for power. In spite of his efforts to avoid "moralizing," McLuhan could not help but condemn "irresponsible" uses of communication techniques in the name of an explicitly fascist power grab.

McLuhan certainly recognized numerous symbolic reinforcements of the unequal relations of power in the everyday lives of Americans. For instance, his essay on "Charlie McCarthy" identifies the voice used by the ventriloquist Edgar Bergen in relation to his dummy Charlie McCarthy as a parrot-like version of corporate and state paternalism riddled with bureaucratese. The distinctive feature of Bergen's voice is a "neutral patience" which for McLuhan "embodies the relationship between the average man and the impersonal agencies of social control in a technological world" (1951: 16). Unfortunately, these agencies remained uninvestigated in McLuhan's work. But at his best he could hear them in the cultural ephemera of the 1950s. It is in this specific sense that there are echoes worth listening to between the *Bride* and *Mythologies*. Still, there always seemed to be something holding McLuhan back. Even his insightful studies of the mechanization and fragmentation of women's bodies in advertising discourses were mired in his distaste for powerful expressions of female sexuality, and treatment of homosexuality and the division between pleasure and procreation as the deleterious effects of the commodification of sex.

It is useful to recall in this context Jonathan Miller's (1971: 76) remarks on McLuhan's "abdication of political intelligence" entailed by his focus on abstract form over content and his celebration of mediatic techniques as examples of avant-gardist practices akin to those used by poets and painters. Miller's reading is astute on the matter of McLuhan's "general ignorance of social reality." Conversely, McLuhan's (1987: 442–44) response to Miller is a masterpiece of professorial paternalism. While the sheer number and variety of political gaffes McLuhan made is in itself astonishing – not to mention the negligible effects the recognition of these have made on contemporary McLuhanites – Miller (1971: 31) acknowledges the important place *The Mechanical Bride* has in cultural criticism.

In *Technology and the Canadian Mind* (1984), Kroker identifies what he calls the first of two "blindspots" in McLuhan's communication theory:

> First, McLuhan had no systematic, or even eclectic, theory of the relationship between economy and technology; and certainly no critical appreciation of the appropriation, and thus privatisation, of technology by the lead institutions, multinational corporations and

the state, in advanced industrial societies. It was not, of course, that
McLuhan was unaware of the relationship of corporate power and
technology. One searing sub-text of *Understanding Media* and *The
Mechanical Bride* had to do with the almost malignant significance of
the corporate control of electronic technologies. . . . But if McLuhan
understood the full dangers of corporate control of technological
media, nowhere did he extend this insight into a reflection on the
relationship of capitalism and technology.

(Kroker 1984: 79)

In short, McLuhan had no political economy of technology and his Catholic
humanism did not contradict "the will to empire." But the "blindspot" of
economy was not exactly a dead spot of political mythology. Kroker rarely
mentions the *Bride* and when he does, it is in virtue of its subtext, albeit a
searing one, a textual maneuver designed to play down the outbursts that run
through McLuhan's text. These very moments of excess are signs of the text
working against itself. Despite Kroker's sympathetic reading of McLuhan – a
rarity, after all, on the left, given the torrents unleashed against him – I want
to draw a different conclusion. Every eruption of political mythology in the
Bride was for McLuhan a step backward into moralizing; yet, in spite
of himself, there are untheorized perceptions of a ubiquitous mythic
consciousness whose influence derives precisely from the ideological fact that
it is represented as the common values of the people. In "Freedom to Listen"
and "Freedom – American Style," McLuhan made an issue of corporate
ownership in America because he witnessed through his study of the mass
media the simulated freedoms permitted to individuals by means of the
practices of consumption.

I am not suggesting that McLuhan had a political mythology of technological consciousness and an insight into the consequences of the ownership
of the means of production. McLuhan's political remarks became reflective
only to the degree that he struggled to achieve the status of a detached and
rational observer who did not "attack" his subject matter. His attempt
to avoid moralizing and erase his point of view did not reveal its own mythic
dimensions through a reflection on his identification with a rational,
detached, paternal and neutral voice, supported by literary allusions. Picking
up on his nautical metaphors, McLuhan taught that students of the mass
media must swim in their waters, practicing so often as to feel at home in
them, if you will. The swimmer who does not experience rough water,
however, has not experienced the power of the medium through which he
moves. The swimmer must be in a position to experience the process by means
of which the medium makes itself strange to him. In this process the medium
reveals its dangers. Applied to the mass media, the image of the whirlpool
implies that there is simply more water around it. This water may be less
turbulent, of course, but it is still water, which is only to say that there was

not, for McLuhan circa 1951, a shoreline in view marking the extent of mass-mediated life. If one cannot simply get out of the water, then one must adapt in order to endure.

Despite the dissimulations and vagaries of the demonstrations of the relationship between McLuhan and Barthes, there remains the matter of the unfulfilled promise of their collaborative effort. "There is no rewind button on the BETAMAX of life," wrote the video artist Nam June Paik (1986: 221) in the course of lamenting that no one had videotaped the periodic meetings of earthly stars such as Cage and McLuhan or even, to add insult to injury for my purposes only, McLuhan and Barthes.

The meetings of McLuhan and Barthes in Paris in 1973 belong to a universe of untaped but not unrealized points of personal contact. These are the stuff of myth or, rather, they are the mythologies of sociologists concerned with sociologists of mythologies, to borrow a reversal used by Pierre Bourdieu and Jean-Claude Passeron (1963: 1006), whose phrases revealed the circular and fantasmagoric logic of French *massmédiologues* for whom "the masses are masses only as the massified receivers [*destinataires*] of a massively diffused mass culture." I shall be careful not to confound the meetings of figures of mythic proportions with myths of their meetings.

Barthes could not be counted among McLuhan's young French readers whose excitement about his ideas seemed to unsettle an older generation of established intellectuals. Moreover, Barthes did not mention McLuhan in his published writings. Conversely, McLuhan mentioned Barthes only in his letters. He appears to have known of *Mythologies* from secondary sources, but he had been made aware by his correspondents of the parallels various critics had found between his and Barthes's early writings on pop culture. Notwithstanding what may be called the "detergent factor" which bound them together – both McLuhan and Barthes recognized the mystical properties afforded to this product, a fact commented upon by both French and English readers alike – their meetings could not generate as much interest in a collaborative project as soap-powder advertisements held for them.

McLuhan and Barthes met at a cocktail party at the apartment of Claude Cartier-Bresson (the former's publisher at Maison Mame) in Paris in the early summer of 1973. McLuhan had flown to Paris on his way to read a paper at the Biennale Internationale de l'Information in Le Touquet, France (June 20, 1973) – (*MP* 137/33, ms., McLuhan, "From Reporting to Programming: The Next One Hundred Years," translated into French by de Kerckhove). Among those present were Cartier-Bresson's well-known brother, the photographer Henri Cartier-Bresson, the sociologist of art Jean Duvignaud, the playwright Eugène Ionesco, the journalist Guy Dumur, the media artist Fred Forest, and McLuhan's friend and colleague in Toronto, Derrick de Kerckhove, as well as an entourage from Mame. As the conversation drifted onto the topic of myth, de Kerckhove, who was acting as a go-between and translator for McLuhan, suggested that the micro-myths of *Mythologies* might give a specific shape to

30

McLuhan's recent thoughts about reworking and updating *The Mechanical Bride*, a book about which he had reservations because he believed it to have been too jejune, too literary, too moralistic, etc. It was McLuhan's enthusiastic French publisher Cartier-Bresson who proffered the idea that McLuhan and Barthes could work at this project together. It is hardly surprising that McLuhan's publisher would suggest such a collaborative effort given the enormous interest it would have generated. A few months after his visit to Paris, Cartier-Bresson wrote to McLuhan inquiring about and expressing his great interest in any projects he may have been working on with Barthes (*MP* 20/81). While McLuhan had initially received the proposal of a collaboration as an amusing idea which might be looked at in more detail, Barthes was willing to entertain it, but with only mild interest. Indeed, the collaborative project was not raised the following day at a meeting over lunch with McLuhan, Cartier-Bresson, Barthes and de Kerckhove. Sensing that the project was doomed, de Kerckhove did not pursue the matter further with McLuhan.[2]

The details of McLuhan's meetings with Barthes neither reinforce the notion that Barthes was "the French McLuhan," nor do McLuhan's remarks on structuralism support the claim that he was a structuralist; it is surely ridiculous to suggest that McLuhan was the "Canadian Barthes." The seductive power of a suggestion at a cocktail party was also at work in the literature of the period, animating the discussion of all those concerned, and driving them to the unstable arrangement of McLuhan and Barthes as potential co-authors. I have been a kind of party pooper in all of this, I admit, having risen to the occasion to isolate an unnoticed correspondence between the two earthly stars on the grounds of their mutual recognition of "bourgeois" consciousness, in their respective countries, as the "common sense" of the period.

McLuhan's *Bride* and Barthes's *Mythologies* belong to a period rich in cultural criticism. In addition to these two ground-breaking books, one may add Richard Hoggart's *The Uses of Literacy* (1957). Together these constitute a strong international trio of cultural studies in the 1950s. This does not mean that cultural studies has its origins in these books of the 1950s. Nonetheless, much can be learned from the evocative literary flavor of their analyses. Anyway, it would be hard to convince those wedded to the Gramscian tradition that cultural studies began with this trio. Stuart Hall (1980:16) was perhaps correct when he wrote of Birmingham school cultural studies that "the search for origins is tempting but illusory."

What is striking about these books of McLuhan, Barthes and Hoggart is the sense of regret each had about the emergence of a mythic consciousness whose distinguishing feature was that it did not want to be identified, and that it erased itself in order to more fully and powerfully perfuse and influence social and cultural life: French bourgeois ideology ex-nominates itself; American magazines offer satisfyingly comprehensive attitudes and opinions to their readers; and the emerging mass form is a "faceless," "classless" and "characterless" culture (Hoggart 1957: 342). Each of these thinkers isolates, with varying degrees of acuity, how the emergence of a self-effacing consciousness steals away the means of self-differentiation and self-definition by making itself the general measure of social being. To be sure, since the writings of McLuhan, Barthes and Hoggart span an impressive political spectrum – Hoggart's "centre socialism" (1992: 90) and Barthes's Marxian-flavored semiology stand apart from McLuhan's struggle for an apolitical objectivity, despite his occasional lapses into cultural critique and his regrets about the sense of regret that slipped through the analyses of the *Bride* – the feeling for what is lost and the consequences of loss differ with each thinker.

Hoggart is strongest on this point. For him, what is lost in the bargain is the cultural character of a class that defined itself in terms of tradition, ritual, myth, community, speech and economic status. Although Hoggart believes that working-class people are remarkably resilient, he places resistance to massification in between passivity and positive response. The British working class endures, Hoggart (1957: 32–33) thinks, because working-class people are not so badly affected by massification as is often thought. This is so "because with a large part of themselves they are just 'not there,' [they] are living elsewhere." But as the faceless culture expands and becomes more invasive, such other psychical sites become fewer and fewer. This was, despite himself, one of the implicit lessons of McLuhan's nautical metaphors: a safe harbor simply couldn't be found. If McLuhan hoped that the study of the mediatic maelstrom would suggest personal strategies for enduring the storm, the more such strategies followed from one's initial capitulation to the very thing with which they sought to deal, the closer endurance moved to the side of passivity born by identification and dependency.

Barthes's lessons were even more abstract. The depoliticized speech of myth enables the social class that does not want to be named to naturalize and eternalize itself. Barthes warned that this was an active political process. He further stipulated, however, that the writing of mythologies, understood as ideological criticism, is not revolutionary since the mythologist is condemned to metalanguage (the seven principal rhetorical forms of myth) while revolution must in the end abolish myth.

Although the work of Barthes is undeniably central to the way we think of cultural studies in the 1950s – this is especially the case with regard to the issue of finding McLuhan's fellow travelers – Barthes was often the odd man out of the trio I have constituted. In other words, French readers of McLuhan such as Pierre-Yves Pétillon (1969) thought of Hoggart rather than of Barthes in the context of assessing McLuhan's contributions to, and place in, the field of analyses concerning the impact of the mass media on contemporary consciousness.

As surprising as this may now seem, it was no more so than what Hoggart himself experienced upon discovering how he was introduced to a French readership. The following passage from the third volume of Hoggart's memoirs, *An Imagined Life: Life and Times*, is worth quoting at length as a point of entry to the French constitution of the Hoggart–McLuhan relationship:

> One English critic, friendly but slightly regretful, described my way of going on as "deceptively descriptive to the point of casualness". I expect he wished to find an explicit pattern of hypotheses, a set of linked generalisations which the individual descriptions supported (as one commonly finds in French writings). But it was a French sociologist, J.-C. Passeron, who, in the introduction to the French edition of *The Uses of Literacy*, suggested – to my surprise – that his countrymen look again at their predilection for theoretical structures and learn something from this English commitment to "phe-nomenological" detail. He did not think my procedure "casual" but, rather, "extraordinarily precise". He even found an "underlying organisation that amounts to an ethnographic inventory".
>
> (Hoggart 1992: 95–96)

Hoggart's *The Uses of Literacy* appeared in French in 1970 under the title of *La culture du pauvre: Etude sur le style de vie des classes populaires en Angleterre*. The title evokes Passeron's impression of detail, precision and ethnographic inventory. The culture of the poor was for Hoggart, one may recall, richer than the emerging classless culture that was transforming English working-class life; comparatively, this new culture was emotionally impoverished. As the economic pressures faced by working-class people were lightened by diverse achievements such as hard-won battles over wages, working conditions and benefits across the bargaining table by the unions for their members, workers faced a new kind of cultural and community "impover-ishment" of meaning against which Hoggart hoped they would endure. What doubly surprised Hoggart was that the English critic was looking for French-style theorizing while the French critic found even less casualness and more inherent structure than Hoggart was prepared to admit – precisely against English cultural expectations!

In his study of the translation, reception and effects of Hoggart's book in France, Rigby (1994: 8) notes an extraordinary irony about the tides of theory:

> It is a rather striking paradox that at the very moment [1971] when English academics were turning to French theorists and delivering unsympathetic judgements on Hoggart's work, a group of French intellectuals, who were themselves destined to become highly regarded, were beginning to hold up Richard Hoggart as an admirable model to follow.

What did McLuhan think of Hoggart? While this question is difficult to answer in detail, a single comment in a letter suffices to sum up McLuhan's attitude: "Hoggart is an utter sap!" (McLuhan 1987: 400). Hoggart was not the sort of fool McLuhan preferred. This rather dismissive remark was provoked by McLuhan's reading of an unsigned *TLS* review, which happened to have been written by a colleague at the Pontifical Institute at the University of Toronto, Brian Stock, of Hoggart's *Speaking to Each Other*. McLuhan was reacting to the idea that television was a vehicle of a faceless and classless culture. As I have argued, McLuhan had long since turned his back on his own version of this critical insight. Such insights were for McLuhan outdated and static, for his exalted position went beyond endorsement and condemnation, or so he believed.

McLuhan's only advance on the Leavisite strategy of the critique of everyday life through the critical analysis of the literature of the canon, was parody (Pétillon 1969: 510). It was a risk that McLuhan took, Pétillon thinks, but lost, since as he descended into the maelstrom, he suffered from an attack of vertigo that disabled his critical faculties. According to Pétillon, in England during the 1950s the study of popular culture displayed a relevance and vibrancy beyond McLuhan's reach in the work of Raymond Williams and others. But for Pétillon, the *"grand nom"* in this field was Hoggart: the research results of the Birmingham Centre for Contemporary Cultural Studies are just as important, but in quite different ways, as those produced at John Culkin's Center for Communications at Fordham, where McLuhan had accepted the Albert Schweitzer chair in 1967–68, bringing along his entourage of Harley Parker and Edmund Carpenter. In a moment of rhetorical excess, Pétillon states that as far as analyses of the impact of the mass media on contemporary consciousness are concerned, "we would give all of McLuhan (except *The Mechanical Bride*) for one chapter of a book by Hoggart" (1969: 510). McLuhan's "intuitions, flashes and fusions" are, on this view, only marginal notes to British cultural studies, and that "it remains to hope . . . that when the dust has settled after its passage, the McLuhan cyclone will have at least been the occasion in France to better discover what there was before and what probably will be after McLuhan" (Pétillon 1969: 511).

Pétillon's approach enables him to place McLuhan in the context of critical moments in the development of cultural studies, but only in order to marginalize his accomplishments by a strategy of exclusion and the rhetorical diminishment of everything he wrote (except the *Bride*) that is not connected to the Birmingham school. As we have seen, McLuhan's readers knocked on the door of structuralism and sought entry for him on the basis of, I tried to show, the vaguest of reasons. McLuhan was shut out in both instances. Still, it is McLuhan's *Bride* that serves as a two-sided signpost, pointing toward both Paris and Birmingham from, of all places, St. Louis.

NOTES

1 McLuhan had read with great interest Jean-Marie Benoist's (1978) book *The Structural Revolution* (London: Weidenfeld & Nicolson), which he described in his own conceptual vocabulary in a letter dated Dec. 19, 1978 to Claude de Beauregard (*MP* 22/17). See also McLuhan's letter to Cleanth Brooks of May 16, 1977 (*MP* 20/22) on structuralism and figure/ground relations.

2 In response to my questions about the meetings of McLuhan and Barthes, Derrick de Kerckhove, director of the McLuhan Program in Culture and Technology at the University of Toronto, generously provided his memories of the events in a conversation in July 1993 in Toronto. Although de Kerckhove's account contradicts McLuhan's brief mention of the episode in his published response to Fulford (that is, McLuhan wrote that "Barthes once asked me . . ."), the idea of a collaborative effort may have at the time been relayed by several willing translators and one very eager publisher, whose genuine excitement at the prospect of such a project may have obscured its precise origin. See also the letter of Claude Cartier-Bresson to McLuhan of July 13, 1973 (*MP* 20/81) and the ms. of de Kerckhove's translation of "From Reporting to Programming: The Next One Hundred Years," presented at the Biennal Internationale de l'Information, Le Touquet, France, June 20, 1973 (*MP* 137/33).

2

THE END OF THE BOOK
AND THE BEGINNING OF
TELEVISION

Alongside prophecy and charlatanry, meteorological phenomena were often used to describe both McLuhan and the effects of his ideas. The "cyclone," to use Pierre-Yves Pétillon's (1969) term, that hit Paris in the mid-1960s was not referred to on a familiar first-name basis, like most North American storms. This wind tore through the capital, rustling the pages of academic and popular publications, and ruffling the feathers of Parisian intellectuals and cultural *animateurs* alike. *Macluhanisme*, as the cyclone came to be known, blew hot and cold or, rather, cool, to borrow McLuhan's concept, depending on how much information one thought it transmitted and, consequently, the degree of participation required to complete its message. But as a lot of hot wind requiring minimal involvement, *macluhanisme* was deflected by those for whom it was fundamentally a loud, albeit beautifully formed, blast. For those who luxuriated in its coolness and the intensive participation it elicited, its dazzle was all the more fascinating and full for the openings it left by flitting from insight to insight. *Macluhanisme* could be unfortunately full but empty, yet gloriously empty but full.

Foul wind or invigorating blast; revolutionary or impostor; *genial Grock*[1] or sinister exaggerator: M(a)cLuhan(isme) was all of these, and more. The cyclone collapsed these disjunctions into a bundle of paradoxes. The study of *macluhanisme* concerns the effects of this phenomenon, its initial explosive impact in the 1960s, and its later lines of influence across French cultural production, particularly in sociological theory broadly conceived. McLuhan himself would not have been entirely pleased with my study of effects, despite the fact that he occasionally claimed to study nothing else. For McLuhan, effects were just as likely to precede causes as vice versa, or occur simultaneously. One first looks for effects and then finds the causes that will produce them; one starts with solutions and creates the problems that they solve.[2] There is some truth in this so-called "artistic strategy," as most marketers know when faced with the situation of having to create needs for a product that satisfies them before they exist, but it should be taken *cum grano salis*, with a grain of salt. The effects of *macluhanisme* are just as paradoxical as its view of effects.

What interests me in this chapter are the places McLuhan's ideas were thought to occupy in French intellectual life. To take a pinch of salt from McLuhan would be to acknowledge that as French thinkers found their bearings in the wake of this cyclone, the effects of *macluhanisme* provided for the invention of a neologism that signified the phenomenon that had hit and continued to batter them. In addition, the place(s) already occupied by this phenomenon had to be found, as it were, in order to explain its sudden and widespread impact on French culture in the first place. These were clean-up operations and justifications rather than examples of non-linear and non-sequential causality. The time was, however, ripe for the arrival of McLuhan's ideas in France for two reasons:

1 the question of *écriture* had already been posed in French philosophical circles, and McLuhan came to be placed in relation to this concept;
2 his emphasis on medium or form over content gave direction to research in the sociology of the media and policy formation in the area of broadcasting.

The intellectual and administrative ambitions of French sociologist Jean Cazeneuve were carried forward on the prevailing winds of *macluhanisme*.

WRITING BEYOND THE BOOK

Not everyone appreciates a cyclone, to say the least. Elaborate defenses against it were mounted as it blew through the human sciences at the Centre d'études des communications de masse of the Ecole pratique des hautes études in Paris.[3] For one of its members, Olivier Burgelin (1969: 1107), not even the abundance of humor found in McLuhan's work could "dispel the tiresome impression of tawdry showiness produced by the incessant handling of overpolished paradoxes." Disrespect for the principle of non-contradiction goes hand-in-hand with a delight in bad puns in McLuhan's imagination. McLuhan's way of being bad troubled Burgelin (1969: 1115) because his "prodigious taste for the new" was really "a greedy acceptance [of it] having nothing to do with intellectual progressivism." This "frantic modernist" seemed unaware that the most contemporary culture of the period was already "out of date, full of the past, of resistance to change, and all sorts of conservatisms," not to mention alienations and anguish (Burgelin 1969: 1116). McLuhan's celebration of modern life rested on a shaky foundation. He "jovially tramples" over ethnography, sociology, linguistics and psycho-analysis, evoking these disciplines only through the names of thinkers from whom he quotes out of context. Burgelin charges that McLuhan doesn't enter into current debates and recent developments in the disciplines from which he borrows. Despite McLuhan's taste for the new, he is out of date and place in every discipline save one: the history of Anglo-Saxon literature in which he was trained. The absence of a semiological reflection on media in McLuhan's work is a case in point for Burgelin; instead of turning toward the sign, McLuhan interests himself in the environments that media constitute, thus weakening, in Burgelin's estimation, the analysis of communication by operating with only two categories of medium/message and content; even here, the latter is understood as another, previously dominant, technological environment (the content of writing is speech; the content of the telephone is the telegraph).

Read today, Burgelin's objections to McLuhan are strikingly anti-postmodern in the sense that they associate him with staple postmodern phenomena such as the confusion of genres and disciplines, the depthlessness of his writing, the poverty of his categories, and impoverishment of his thematics by his own incessant punning.

Burgelin advises that McLuhan cannot be "read to the letter." For example, while causality is the single explanatory principle expressing the relationship between media and galactic shifts in history, the use of this concept is largely metaphorical and signifies congruence, significantly reducing the power of the analysis. "McLuhan's system has no scientific value," Burgelin states (1969: 1110–11), and for this reason the empirical validity of research in the sociology of mass media makes as little sense to McLuhan as McLuhan's "results" make for such a breed of sociologist. Indeed, Burgelin (1969: 1112) makes the important passing observation that McLuhan's response to the necessity of empirical validation is that this requirement "dissimulates the true problems, a little like rationalisation in the Freudian sense." This places McLuhan in the position of the analyst for whom the figurative analysand, an empirically minded sociologist of media, subjects the media to an explanatory principle, including a strong appeal to "reality," which conceals the unconscious motives and defenses of the analysand's methodological claim. Rationalization in this context is a form of resistance to McLuhan's efforts to understand the "true" structure of the medium as message. This is the first intimation of the psychological profile of the paradoxes into which one was plunged by voicing criticisms of McLuhan. I take up this issue in more detail in Chapter 3.

The "idea that communication does not exhaust itself in the manifest content of the message" is for Burgelin (1969: 1114) McLuhan's most general and enduring insight. This did not, however, align McLuhan with a depth hermeneutics. If for many French thinkers McLuhan's focus on the medium put him into contact with structuralism – a matter I considered in some depth in the previous chapter – it also enabled him to be placed in relation to the sorts of poststructuralism practiced by Barthes, Derrida and the group around the journal *Tel Quel*. This placement is from the outset extraordinarily awkward since, as Burgelin himself admits (1969: 1114), "McLuhan ignores and apparently contradicts them." Jean Texier (1968) had, in a similar spirit, suggested that McLuhan's "annihilation of *écriture*" should be the occasion to turn our attention to the "real research" of Barthes and Derrida. This placement which resists the very gesture, thereby working against itself, is made to work on the basis of the shared problematization of the oppositional and metaphysical concepts of speech and writing. Burgelin's readers are left to recall that the double gesture of Derridean deconstruction overturns and displaces the hierarchical arrangement of such metaphysical oppositions in order to analyze hitherto subordinated aspects of the inferior concept of writing, releasing, in order to graft them onto a new, general concept of writing (Derrida 1982: 329–30). The speech/writing opposition is central to McLuhan's understanding of the transition from the scribal galaxy to the new oral society. But this transition or passage from one concept to the other is not, Derrida specifies, the way of deconstruction. Still, Burgelin (1969: 1114) insists:

> However, it is the same value that is sought, despite the contradiction of the formulations, here under the denomination of *écriture*, there under that of medium, and, more clearly, it is a similar conception of signification that is rejected here as speech, and there as content. In both cases, what is foregrounded is that communication cannot be reduced to the single signified of the message.

The rhetorical promise by default of a *rapprochement* between Derrida and McLuhan in terms of the speech/writing opposition wanes as we read Derrida's (1982: 329) first concluding remark in "Signature Event Context" from *Margins of Philosophy*: "We are not witnessing an end of writing which, to follow McLuhan's ideological representation, would restore a transparency or immediacy of social relations . . ." Instead, Derrida continues, emphasizing his own accomplishment, "but indeed a more and more powerful historical unfolding of a general writing of which the system of speech, consciousness, meaning, presence, truth, etc., would only be an effect, to be analyzed as such." Derrida rejects McLuhan's vision of the psychological and social wholeness of pre- and post-literate cultures. His rejection is less interesting than the avenue it opens: the liberation and generalization of the hitherto subordinated predicates of writing. The movement toward the general is parallel to McLuhan's abandonment of specialism, separation, continuity, uniformity, homogeneity (all of the effects of the phonetic alphabet) toward the "web" (McLuhan 1964: 86) of orality, what Fekete (1982: 63), in his discussion of the passage from Derrida cited above, called "a general oral form." Fekete leaves the task of working out the relationship between these two generalities (writing and orality) to future scholars. However, he does so ahistorically, that is, without recognizing the history of the relationship between McLuhan and Derrida already worked through during McLuhan's French reception. This does not lessen the significance of the question Fekete posed, nor lessen the degree of difficulty of the task he bequeathed us. The question I wish to pose concerns the general oral form: is there anything that prevents it from being one of those "effects" of which Derrida wrote above? To put it in slightly different terms: is there anything that prevents the general oral form from being logocentric? My answer is no.

In France during the late 1960s, Derrida's name was regularly invoked in discussions of McLuhan's concept of writing for the sake of diminishing the seriousness of the latter's work. This is evident in François Châtelet's (1967: 37) claim that despite the "absurdity" and "deliberately fraudulent" nature of McLuhan's theories, they are "not without relation to the true questions." In this backhanded way, then, Châtelet (1967: 37) continues:

> For it is correct that culture and its diffusion are currently under-going a radical mutation and that the primacy of the book is being contested. This new situation requires a deep reflection on the fact of writing, reading and the precarious imperialism of discourse.

And for Châtelet it is Derrida who has reflected most deeply and seriously on these matters. McLuhan is a *faiseur* (a word meaning both a shark and a show-off, among other things) and the "pretentious foolishness" of *macluhanisme* threatens France. Châtelet does not specify the precise nature of the threat, but it is surely a question of resisting the schemes of a concept-shark. Perhaps Châtelet believed that he was protecting the youth of France against the seductions of a pseudo-theory. This move, incidentally, is precisely the one that convicted Socrates, and it is also the one used most commonly by conservative American critics with reference to Baudrillard. Sullen American conservatives and reactionary French philosophers alike would have both McLuhan and Baudrillard drink their respective cups of hemlock.

Jean-Marie Benoist (1968: 4) pointed out that McLuhan thought "the electronic media restore a space of plenitude and presence"; that is, in McLuhan's writing the transition from writing to speech is logocentric and entails transparency, immediacy, nowness and presence on a global scale. This is precisely what Derrida objects to as "ideological." McLuhan's oral society is, however, marked by an "acoustic orientation" that is also tactile or auditive-tactile. What this means is that orality is irreducible to speech as such because tactility is for McLuhan a sign of the interplay of the senses, itself irreducible to haptic sensation. This does not make McLuhan's oral culture any less metaphysical, it is just that care must be taken in the application of its predicates. My negative answer has, then, one qualification. McLuhan's knowledge of the writings of Derrida was extremely limited. His reading of Derrida was mediated by the writings of Roger Poole, Professor of English at the University of Nottingham. In the late 1970s, Poole was a Visiting Commonwealth Fellow at York University in Toronto and during his stay sent McLuhan several mansucripts (*MP* 193/29, 193/30), including his review of Derrida's *Of Grammatology*. From these articles McLuhan familiarized himself with the term deconstruction, the activities of the Yale Derrideans, and could not resist a pun on Derrida's name, "Deride," which he scribbled in the margins of Poole's review. Poole left McLuhan with the incorrect impression that deconstruction was only a negative project, a single, derisive gesture, as it were.

Although the passage into a generalized orality is part of a "euphoric ideology," in Edgar Morin's (1969:18) words, that holds little interest for deconstruction, this aspect is precisely what interests others. Morin had many regrets about *macluhanisme*, including the reduction of a "gigantic historical period to a single and monotone factor . . . a technological medium." Morin (1969: 16) writes: "If the paradigm of McLuhan is poor, his syntagm is rich, not only in terms of the flux of the proposed contiguities, but as much by a dialectical sense, sometimes light, sometimes subtle." McLuhan's galactic thought can be subtle and supple despite its "schematic dogmatism," since it alerts us to the interpenetration of galaxies and the neo-tribal or neo-archaic elements of neo-modernity. While Morin (1968: 16) valued the flexibility of McLuhan's "galactic way of thinking, i.e., one which strives to establish large configurations where unexpected associations reveal a flexible search after complex structuration," the conceptual sensurround of *macluhanisme* just as easily produced a galactic giddiness.

Suffice to say that the place of *macluhanisme* was generally recognized as the philosophical milieu in which the deconstruction of the speech/writing opposition took place. It is the work of the grammatologist Derrida, however, that is said to be both real and true. To this depth McLuhan could only pretend and display the surface effects of serious thinking. The end of the book is not, for McLuhan, the beginning of writing, of Derridean *écriture*. The end of the book is the beginning of television. McLuhan thought that writing was a supplement to speech; in fact, it was sandwiched between two oralities, the first originary and the second neo-originary, whose unity it interrupted. For writing separates and specializes and undoes the "tribal web" by granting the individual emotional freedom (McLuhan 1964: 82–84); it is also civilizing, intensifying, visual and uniform. In short, writing is exterior to the speech whose place it takes and keeps, and this belief placed McLuhan firmly in the Western metaphysical tradition as Derrida represents it. Derrida (1974: 313, 315) takes the "risk," then, in *Of Grammatology*, of thinking of writing as an originary supplement that takes place *before* and *within* speech. What makes this thought risky is that it seems absurd and totally unacceptable within the tradition that separates the source from the supplement, a separation McLuhan does nothing to challenge.

THE EMPIRE OF CAZENEUVE

In the midst of these debates, Cazeneuve was slowly building his own empire of communications by turning *macluhanisme* toward the formation of state policy. Cazeneuve's (1976) entry under the neologism *macluhanisme* in *Les communications de masse: Guide alphabétique* produced under his direction begins with the claim that McLuhan stands apart from all those who have written on the mass media. Not only does the neologism bear his name, but McLuhan's audience is the largest in the field and his writings are the most widely contested. It is the prophetic character of McLuhan's thought that makes it subject to criticisms based upon its lack of scientific rigor. Even if the directions in which McLuhan pushed discussions may be turned against his initial signposts, no matter, Cazeneuve suggests, since controversy is what makes McLuhan's ideas resonate even louder.

Of the three pillars of *macluhanisme* (the triumph of medium over content; the opposition of hot and cool media; the technological determination of civilizational transformation) the first "accomplished a kind of Copernican revolution" (Cazeneuve 1976: 260) in media studies. The study of content or the effects of messages gave way to the consideration of the effects of media as forms of communicational interaction of which there are two broad types (hot and cool). No matter how "artificial" this typology may be in practice, it does not detract from the sociological and prophetic significance of the third pillar. What fascinates Cazeneuve (1976: 265) is the sociological issue of cultural mutation that *macluhanisme* captures in terms of the interpenetration of *la galaxie Gutenberg* and our own post-literate galaxy. As far as Copernican revolutions are concerned, there have been several notable ones, namely those of Darwin with regard to anthropocentric consciousness and consciousness as such with Freud (McLuhan 1967: 363). The universe in question or, rather, the galactic sensibility attuned to content, was an influential one (albeit relatively small in planetary terms!) in the expanding universe of mass communications. If Gutenberg put the reader at the center of the universe of knowledge delivered by print culture, then McLuhan indicated the field created by electric-electronic networks in which the individual point of view of the private reader would inhere and break down, even if he taught this lesson through the products of alphabetic culture, namely, books.

For Cazeneuve (1976: 265), *macluhanisme* points toward a socially harmonious future in which the crises engendered by overlapping galaxies are surmounted by embracing new systems of media, while renouncing those born of the Gutenberg era. Much more than Morin, then, Cazeneuve was cooled – in its salutary sense – by *macluhanisme*: "One must not ask oneself if *macluhanisme* is serious; one must play its game and take note of what it reveals about the world of tomorrow" (Cazeneuve 1969b: 7). What if the very technological breakthroughs *macluhanisme* tells us to embrace have the residual effect of creating social disharmony through, for instance, economic instability and intergenerational strife arising from proximity and inter-connectedness? Intergenerational injustice of the kind felt by "Generation X" and the Baby-Boomers is congruent with the tensions of overlapping galaxies, even if the latter are defined generationally rather than technologically (still, demography and its mutant offspring such as psychography are tools of marketing).

Cazeneuve's alphabetic guide was not written according to critical issues or problems. *Macluhanisme* was given free rein, for example, in Hervé Fischer's contribution on the esthetics of mass media (in Cazeneuve 1976: 203–14). *Macluhanien* distinctions are employed in the dual service of the search for a definition of an esthetics of electronic (primarily televisual) images, and in the exploration of the notion of an *écriture télévisuelle*, an electronic rhetoric of camerawork and editing that transcends the commonplace consumption of the semantic signs of realism found in reportage. De Kerckhove (1986: 49, 51) has developed this esthetic approach by contrasting the effects of filmic editing to televisual modulation; in the case of films shown on television, the harsher images and intense motion of the former are softened by the gentle waves of color and light of the latter. In order to appreciate the extent of Cazeneuve's engagement with *macluhanisme*, it is necessary to turn to his earlier writings on cultural mutations and the mass media.

In "Communications de masse et mutations culturelles," Cazeneuve writes: "*Macluhanisme* is a fashion, a craze that unmakes intellectual beds and reaches the general public" (1969a: 17). Focussing on the third phase of the third pillar of *macluhanisme* (the return of an oral culture in the electronic civilization), Cazeneuve accepts the analysis of the sensorial mutations (visual bias) of alphabetic man, but considers the claim for a new orality to be a debatable point. It seems that "the mass media are audio-visual means, and perhaps even more and more visual" (1969a: 22). Cazeneuve maintains that "although [McLuhan] sometimes clearly confirms that the mass media lead to the primacy of the oral and the auditory, at other moments he seems to indicate that we are leaning instead towards an equilibrium between vision and hearing" (1969a: 22). The visual bias of electronic media and the not particularly difficult task of finding ambiguous statements of position by McLuhan led Cazeneuve to suggest that current cultural mutations cannot be characterized by "the reflux of the visual and the return of the oral" (1969a: 22). Later in the article Cazeneuve rephrases and hedges his position: "Thus, it is probably, contrary to what McLuhan understood, the reinforcement of the visual that is the most remarkable cultural effect of the mass media" (1969a: 24).

Cazeneuve in addition argues that McLuhan did not pay sufficient attention to the ways in which the mass media transform culture into commodities that become more and more ephemeral. Broadcasts are, he thinks, less permanent than books. In the era before zapping and videorecorders, Cazeneuve reminds us, broadcasts received in the home could not be taped and replayed, stopped and edited. Ultimately, Cazeneuve is prepared to let *macluhanisme* off the hook, since its exaggerations in the area of sensorial mutations are balanced by the attention it focusses on new media and the conceptual equipment it provides for their interpretation.

In his review of the French translations of McLuhan's work available in 1969 (*La galaxie Gutenberg* (1967), *Message et massage* (with Fiore 1968b), *Pour comprendre les médias* (1968a), *Mutations 1990* (1969f)), Cazeneuve (in collaboration with Gérard Namer 1969: 140) reflects on the "promotion of [McLuhan] to the rank of a big star." It may be the case that in North America "the only type of reaction that this oeuvre has not provoked is precisely indifference." In France reactions have been mixed: "the public was not staggered, and sociologists, by and large, did not let go of their defiant, and at times contemptuous attitude" (Cazeneuve and Namer 1969: 140). This so-called mixed response is perhaps due to, Cazeneuve conjectures, the fact that the elements of surprise, shock, diversion, word play and the rambling remarks of McLuhan "are not the sort that greatly move the Latin character." This sort of posturing on the side of Latinity snubs North American boosterism and special effects from which the "Latin character" is stereotypically and mythically immune, despite much evidence in postwar French writing to the contrary. Cazeneuve and Namer throw up a rickety windscreen against the blasts of *macluhanisme*.

McLuhan does not, Cazeneuve and Namer (1969: 141) lament, pick up in *Pour comprendre les médias* where he left off in *La galaxie Gutenberg*. He develops neither his views on the primitive pre-Gutenberg era nor of print culture but, instead, "they operate only as a means of reference or of comparison." Cazeneuve and Namer go so far as to refer to developments in *Pour comprendre* regarding the analysis of the specific effects of communications technologies as work on *mass media* – a term, they comment disparagingly, that belongs to "the barbaric language of specialists." By this criterion alone, McLuhan, Cazeneuve and Namer are barbarians! With the arrival of *Mutations 1990*, McLuhan is in full prophetic mode and abandons himself to "sociological fiction." Cazeneuve mishandles McLuhan's typological distinction between cool and hot by first correctly including radio and cinema among hot media, and later incorrectly referring to them as cool (in contrast to television!) (Cazeneuve and Namer 1969: 145). Unwittingly, then, Cazeneuve provides evidence for his claim that this typological distinction has not always been understood in the world of broadcasting, the very place where he distinguished himself in the 1960s and 1970s in a series of administrative roles, including those of Administrateur de l'Office de radiodiffusion-télévision française (ORTF 1964–70; 1972–74), Président du Comité des programmes de la télévision à l'ORTF (1971–74), and Président-directeur général et fondateur de la Société nationale de télévision de la première chaîne (TF1) (1974–78).

What is Cazeneuve's legacy? His work is not widely read today. But his various explications and soft interrogations of McLuhan were perfectly adapted to the debates over form and content under way in France in the 1960s and 1970s, especially in relation to a fledgling media studies interested in content. By appealing to McLuhan's so-called revolution of form against vaguely leftist notions of revolutionizing the content of media, Cazeneuve was able to adopt a passively critical stance, even if his position aligned itself with technological determinism, and effectively released himself from the demands of the critiques of Marxism and *macluhanisme*. In short, Cazeneuve was one of the first occupants of a largely vacant space that existed in the study of television in France in the 1960s and 1970s.

As Michèle and Armand Mattelart explain (1990: 112–13; 121, n. 12), two factors contributed to the rise of *macluhanisme* in France. First, the field of television remained undertheorized almost until the 1980s and, second, the antinomy of form and content produced a "theoretical vacuum" into which *macluhanisme* swept and subsequently "exercised its power of seduction." Armand Mattelart and Yves Stourdzé (1985: 80) have cited the work of McLuhan as the prime example of "trans-historic discourses which cannot hide their occultation, not only of the real as it appears on television, but of the real, full stop." On this view, the credibility afforded to McLuhan was one of the unfortunate political effects of the "intellectual underdevelopment" of the study of television. Moreover, without "serious scientific analysis of the material mode of functioning" to offset its emergence, *macluhanisme* could be "called to the rescue to paper over the cracks of a society which generally refused to think of television as the matrix of its system of modern communication, as the central mechanism for the production of consensus" (Mattelart and Stourdzé 1985: 80). This explanation of McLuhan's influence in France relies on the description of the theoretical scene of writing on television as immature and empty, and figures McLuhan's work as seductive in the sense that it draws attention away from the real into the irreal or a rhetorically devalued realm, and does so by papering over and thereby occluding substantive insights into the social influence of television, which was precisely the situation that Cazeneuve so brilliantly exploited.

It is worth citing at length Jean-Marie Piemme's critique of the wooly "theoretical foundations of the dominant discourse on television" to which Mattelart and Stourdzé refer, since Cazeneuve is one of the agents whose writings and administrative positions supposedly obstructed communications research in France:

> In France, there exists a discourse on the subject of television, and more generally, on mass communications, whose very fame makes it impossible to ignore. It emanates from Jean Cazeneuve, long known for several books and even more articles on television and the mass media. His writings have a certain audience and his opinions on this subject are regularly solicited as much by journalists and newspapers as, more recently, by public authorities. His expert knowledge of the

problems of television has led him not only to be the sociologist that he is, but also, at the request of the Giscardian regime, to take over the first television channel. This ultimate promotion is not the least of the reasons for examining his central thesis more closely.

The books of Jean Cazeneuve have the particularity of taking on the appearance of being the sum total of all that has been said on the subject. References to work of all shades abound and analyses make imperturbable use of any empirical study with a few results to flaunt. Drawing mainly on American and Anglo-Saxon authors, Cazeneuve, according to the needs of his panorama, adds the results of often irreconcilable theories, corrects results of one study by the results of another, to which he generally adds the results of a third, and takes what he needs from psychology, empirical mass-media sociology, social psychology and the functionalist approach. He goes from Gurevitch to McLuhan by passing through the evolutionist thinkers of the nineteenth century, makes more references to Jung than to Freud and bases all his reflections on a certain idea of man and the human condition.

(Piemme, quoted in Mattelart and Stourdzé 1985: 82)

In short, Cazeneuve's eclecticism is a McLuhanist veneer. But for Mattelart and Stourdzé, Cazeneuve's eclecticism lacks McLuhan's originality, and he fails to consolidate the multiple positions from which he speaks. Cazeneuve's construction of television by the arrangement of irreconcilable theories enabled his point of view to hide among the flecks of his imperfect mosaic method. His position was mobile, fluent and apparently liberal enough to move over to the side of the object of his interest, especially in the era of Giscardian liberalism. Recall that McLuhan admired the liberal politics of Valéry Giscard d'Estaing in France, Jerry Brown in California and Pierre Trudeau in Canada.

It was during Cazeneuve's tenure (but not directorship) in the ORTF that opposition to the introduction of advertising on television finally weakened sufficiently to allow it entry onto the little French screen. After the print media had staved off repeated attempts in the 1960s (1960, 1962, 1965) to institute de Gaulle's demand for television commercials on economic grounds, in 1968 the event occurred (Thibau 1970: 152–54), although limitations were placed on the duration of adverts, and an independent organ (Régie française de publicité (RFP)) was established to control the excesses of private interests by ensuring that revenue from advertising did not exceed 25 percent of public resources, and limit the duration of advertising time. Created in 1969, the RFP was disbanded in 1992 (Cazeneuve was not the director of the ORTF during the eruption of televisual publicity; it was a certain Monsieur E. Biasini who made the decision in 1967). The tumultuous year of 1968 may have brought students and workers onto the streets, but it

46

also brought commercials and color to television. According to Jean-Louis Missika and Dominique Wolton (1983: 52ff.), the events of May 1968 revealed the repressive and paternalistic dimensions of the "statist model" of television and the control over culture and information it exercised, given the government's decision not to speak to the events on television and suppress what were considered to be subversive reports. It was not until the election of Georges Pompidou in 1969 that, on this view, the liberalization of French television began to occur. Missika and Wolton (1983: 179, 294) resist both McLuhan's and Cazeneuve's techno-prophecies of television in the planetary age on the grounds that the medium will not blur the distinction between totalitarian and liberal controls on the basis of its alleged receptivity to public opinion and contemporary events; it has not operated without restrictions and is unlikely to achieve transparency, as the French case has (Missika and Wolton contend) demonstrated.

References to the professionalization of McLuhan's slogan "the medium is the message" translate into policy statements in this way: if the user of a medium is its content, as McLuhan came to believe, then there is no barrier to the introduction of commercials to television (nor to the importation of programs), since no significant change occurs to the medium with their appearance. Wherever the blame is laid for the introduction of the good news of multinational capital to French television, it would not be the last time that *macluhanisme* would be used to influence and justify policy decisions. McLuhan's own interventions in this area are well known in Canada. "We are the content of anything we use, if only because these things are extensions of ourselves," McLuhan (1987: 427) wrote in a letter to Jim Davey, program secretary in the Office of the Prime Minister in Trudeau's government. It followed for McLuhan that the CRTC (Canadian Radio and Telecom-munications Commission) policy requiring a certain percentage of Canadian content in broadcasting was based on a misunderstanding of the media. The "user as content" supplement to the slogan "the medium is the message" means that Canadians are the content of the American media they use (or the French are the content of the American media they consume), and thus a policy aimed at limiting American (and, in general, transborder) access to the Canadian market and promoting Canadian cultural productions is ill-conceived and unnecessary – a residual effect of the Gutenberg galaxy and its misguided nationalism and protectionism.

Throughout the 1970s McLuhan advanced this line of thinking on a variety of fronts, none of which proved to be particularly influential in the explicit formation of broadcasting policy in Canada at the time, much to his chagrin (this is evident in his unpublished correspondence from 1971 with John Bassett, chairman and publisher of the defunct newspaper *The Toronto Telegram*; see *MP* 18/80). Today, both French and Canadian struggles against American imports are simply being left behind by satellite technologies which effectively ignore national boundaries. McLuhan was correct that new technologies wreak havoc with old regulatory regimes. His stance against Canadian content rules was not, he believed, a political position at all but, rather, an instance of his exalted position beyond endorsement and condemnation that was informed by attention to the medium itself. He was very much alone with his uncritical followers in this belief.

The cyclone of *macluhanisme* neither blew itself out in the awkward comparisons of Derrida and McLuhan that quickly took on contrasting tones, nor did the occasional xenophobic outbursts warning France of its dangers provide much shelter; neither was it exhausted in the opportunities for self-promotion that it afforded those such as Cazeneuve in the sociology and adminstration of the mass media in France. By way of a conclusion, however, let's consider one of the positive contributions that *macluhanisme* was thought to have made to poststructuralist critique.

IS LANGUAGE ELECTRIC?

In *Anti-Oedipus*, Deleuze and Guattari (1977: 240) ask: "What exactly is meant when someone announces the collapse of the 'Gutenberg galaxy'?" The answer to this question concerns the role of *macluhanisme* in the schizophrenic process and anarchic anoedipalism. McLuhan's announcement at first seems puzzling since capitalism, despite what Deleuze and Guattari think about its "profound illiteracy," still uses writing and communicates through it as printed money, for example. What happens to writing in the age of "electric language"? Does the electric revolution come to language in a way that is irreducible to the orality that takes one back to the source?

Deleuze and Guattari (1977: 240) continue: "This seems to us to be the significance of McLuhan's analysis: to have shown what a language of decoded flows is, as opposed to a signifier that strangles and overcodes the flows." Without a despotic signifier that holds the signified in the straitjacket of an asymmetrical dichotomy and codes it relationally in a closed system of oppositions, no single flow (libidinal energy or electric transmissions) can control the fluxes and constellations of desire whose connectivity is prodigious. Signification is structured, coded, controlled. Hence, Deleuze and Guattari appeal to television signals (ironically, the code of *multiplexage analogique de composantes* (MAC), unlike SECAM (*Séquentiel couleur à mémoire*) or PAL (Phase Alternative Line), raises the question of how we are to understand the French spelling of McLuhan's name as *Mac*Luhan, a matter to which I turn in Chapter 3) and the pure information of the electric light as examples of decoded flows. The decoded flow of the electric light, Deleuze and Guattari suggest, forms a substance "by entering into a relationship with another flow, such that the first defines a content and the second, an expression" (1977: 241).

Deleuze and Guattari graft the categories of Louis Hjelmslev's glossematics onto McLuhan's concept of the electric light, understood as a contentless and messageless medium of communication that can enter into a relationship that is neither predetermined nor determinable, forming a substance (a decoded flow is unformed matter that is given form, thereby becoming a substance). The meeting of flows creates, in other words, meaning. But the relation between content and expression is relative and reversible, which explains why there is no dominant signifier and no predeterminable hierarchy. Remember that this is the part of the *Anti-Oedipus* in which a strange trio appears: McLuhan, Hjelmslev and Jean-François Lyotard.[4] Certain concepts from each thinker (electric light as pure information; content–expression–form–substance; the figural) are favorably evaluated on the basis of their contributions to the critique of the signifier. McLuhan specifies (1964: 9) that the content may "blind" one to the medium, but it need not do so, since "content or uses of such media are as diverse as they are ineffectual in shaping the form of human association." Electric light is pure information, a plane of immanence in which no one knows what sorts of relationships will be established, set in motion by the capitalist production of power and the sale of electricity. Electric light is, after all, salable, and it is this feature that allows the capitalist code to determine its flow through the circuits it builds and owns, and rents. For Deleuze and Guattari capitalism at the same time decodes and limits by encoding the flows it releases.

A fly in the ointment of Deleuze and Guattari's recuperation of McLuhan is that schizophrenia, as one finds in *The Gutenberg Galaxy* (1962: 22), is a consequence of literacy (specifically, the phonetic alphabet), not of the new orality. The split at issue is between ear and eye, and it breeds separation and dichotomania. McLuhan's usage is closer to Deleuze and Guattari's references to schizophrenia as a clinical entity than to their sense of it as a process entailing breakthroughs rather than breakdowns.

What is electric language? "Electric language does not go by way of the voice or writing," Deleuze and Guattari write (1977: 241), echoing McLuhan's dream of a generalized decoding without verbalization: beyond language is the decoding machine, the computer, and beyond its promise of a "Pentecostal condition of universal understanding and unity" achieved by means of instantaneous translation, there is the "general cosmic conscious-ness": a condition of "speechlessness [and signlessness] that could confer a perpetuity of collective harmony and peace" (McLuhan 1964: 84). The sempiternal glance of angels is an asemiotic state of perfect and instant communication. How important, then, can McLuhan's thinking be for the critique of the signifier and schizoanalysis if it actually relies upon a transcendental signifier, whose despotic influence, Deleuze and Guattari hoped, they would escape, by establishing a field of immanence? And what about the metaphysical speech/writing opposition that McLuhan reinforces, despite this religious vision which dissolves the generalized orality, already contaminated in the mundane world by haptic sensations? It alone should suffice to dampen Deleuze and Guattari's spirited support for this aspect of

McLuhan's thought since only the destruction of this old binarism wins their praise. Deleuze and Guattari exercise the interpretive freedom to pick and choose and transform the ideas they borrow without respecting the contexts from whence they came. They make McLuhan radical for their own ends regardless of what in his thought, as I have suggested, may militate against their creative borrowings. It takes a lot of imagination to make *macluhanisme* radical.

NOTES

1 This obscure reference is to Adrien Wettach Grock (1880–1959), the Swiss circus performer (acrobat and musician closely associated with the violin and piano he used as props). Grock and his partner Brick were well known in France. Grock performed across Europe, England and North Africa for over 50 years. The phrase was used by Alain Vernay (1969) "La galaxie Gutenberg ou le prophète McLuhan," *Le Figaro* (Jan. 25).

2 McLuhan wrote: "This artistic strategy is indispensable today: you start with the solution and then you create the problem that will lead to that solution. Or, you start with the effect and then you look for the situations that will produce that effect. The nineteenth-century approach was the reverse of this. It is the approach of heavy industry and consumer-oriented minds today – start with the problem, then look for the solution. This is fine for a society enveloped by information moving at a slow rate. At high speeds, on the other hand, every solution creates more problems than it can resolve" ("Media and the Structured Society," *The McLuhan Dew-Line Newsletter* 2/1 (July 1969c): 3). The reversal of cause and effect is part of a larger rhetoric of reversal or flip that takes place when a thing has reached a point of exhaustion or saturation. This reversal is tied to the implosive speed of new information technologies. This implosive speed, in turn, makes the item-by-item processing of information impossible or at least redundant, requiring a new kind of awareness adequate to the field of perception; hence, for McLuhan, what he called audile-tactile synesthesia.

3 The Centre d'études des communications de masse (CECMAS) was founded by Georges Freidmann in 1960 at the Ecole pratique des hautes études, then under the direction of Fernand Braudel. Burgelin was an active member of the Centre. The semio-structural method favored by its early and most distinguished members such as Barthes, Metz and Todorov in the 1960s, opened onto post-structural speculation with the arrival of Kristeva, the emergence of Baudrillard, and the confusion of methods in general that marked the 1970s. During 1972–73, CECMAS became CETSAS, the Centre d'études transdisciplinaires. This is not to downplay the sociological perspective Freidmann, Paul Lazarsfeld and Edgar Morin, among others, brought to the study of mass media.

4 The trio of McLuhan–Hjelmslev–Lyotard constitutes, for Deleuze and Guattari, a critique of point of view. For McLuhan, as he explained in *The Gutenberg Galaxy* (1962), the orality of the electronic age undermines closed systems of alphabetic and typographic culture (specifically, a fixed point of view) and creates an interplay between modes of perception. Lyotard would call this the libidinal-esthetic

force of the figural which disrupts closed discursive systems, and displaces any fixed "point of view" or identity. The fluidity of the figural also makes it irreducible to the visual, which in McLuhan's terms is consonant with the critique of vision in terms of acoustic space. But the discursive, in Lyotard's deconstruction of the discourse/figure opposition, also inhabits the space of the figural, just as in McLuhan, the Gutenberg legacy lingers in today's acoustic space. The result is "trauma and tension."

3

MAC

There was a moment, or many of them, in the French reception of the writings of McLuhan, in which his views were revealed to be a *trompe l'oeil* splashed across the mediascape. As the gaze of his admirers shifted after an initial wide-eyed fixation, they noticed that McLuhan's views did not move with their own. These views appeared as something other than they seemed, or rather they now seemed to be something else, to paraphrase Jacques Lacan (1977a: 112). This other thing was the *objet petit a*.

I have just imagined the moment(s) in which McLuhan became MacLuhan for his French readers with the help of an extra little *a*. If this imagining is too hard to swallow, it is all for the better since the *objet petit a* is, Lacan notes, hard to swallow. As the loving stares of M(a)cLuhan's French readers broke away from their precious object, I would like to think they did so in terms similar to those Lacan used in describing the relation between analysand and analyst: the love transference hung on something more than the analyst had, and the analysand's gift of love turned out to be a load of shit (Lacan 1977a: 268). There is very little difference between the *objet petit a* and the *objet petit tas*, as Lacan once punned. The Lacanian concept of the *objet petit a* will help us to understand the meaning MacLuhan had for his French readers, especially those who insisted on spelling his name in this manner, a phenomenon that took place in France but not Québec. The word "reader" is already problematic, since one of the things Lacan and McLuhan had in common was television.

If my very premiss here appears suspect — that there is something in the matter of the "French spelling" of M(a)cLuhan — I can only offer a justification, after the fact, based on anecdote. A certain sociological theorist, a postmodernist, no less, recently seized upon the rendering of the phenomenon of *macluhanisme* in the title of one of my recently published articles as if it were an invention of my own; to this spelling he added "*sic*." Did he mean strange or incorrect? I did not invent it, strange as this may seem. Whether this was a comment on my French I will probably never know. The spelling was intentional, and this chapter attempts to theorize it. For me, what makes this banal act of mistaken "correction" interesting is this: why was my reader compelled to add a little more to the addition?

Both Lacan and McLuhan appeared on "primal time television" broadcasts, to use a phrase coined by Lawrence Rickels, in France in the early 1970s. While Lacan's appearance may have alarmed certain bookish Lacanians, who feared that by massaging the masses psychoanalysis said nothing at all, Lacan himself spoke in the name of "non-idiots" (analysts) and, presumably, "idiots" (non-analysts) as well. If it didn't make a difference to Lacan that he spoke in the name of the "public" before the blackboard in his seminar or the couch potatoes – no pun intended! – glued to their television screens, it was because he addressed neither of their gazes, which he claimed were really only one. But this is just the sort of difference upon which McLuhan's media theory rested. To be fair to Lacan, he recognized that the mass media had psychical effects linked to technological developments, a lesson he learned and adapted brilliantly by appeals to a variety of media, not from McLuhan, but from "Freud's analogical hook-up of technology and the unconscious" (Rickels 1990: 43). For Lacan, McLuhan's mediatic extensions of man could not account for what was more than themselves.

MacSPELL

McLuhan's great-grandfather William McLughan arrived in Essa Township in the Province of Ontario, Canada, from County Down, Ireland, in 1849 and began his life in Canada with a new, shortened name: McLuhan. This change of family name was not an uncommon practice in the nineteenth and even twentieth centuries, for Canadian immigration officers have, with every new wave of immigrants, indulged in the disfiguration of names, not to mention families. Having lost a letter from his family name, McLuhan would ultimately gain another, albeit a different one, from many of his French readers for whom a certain "MacLuhan" appeared, at least at first in certain circles, as a prophet of sorts. This rendering was not an overt attempt at some kind of Franco-Scots-Irish amalgamation, according to which the little imported *a* would signify an international family affair. Taken on its face value, the little *a* filled a perceived gap between *M* and *c* for the delicate French ear, for which a little thing, already worming its way into pronunciation, would smooth over a ragged, foreign construction uncommon in French. For this reason, then, "MacLuhan" is in a way a Gallicized version of "McLuhan," even if the very gesture makes it foreign. But it is not without its confusions since, on the one hand, "Mac" means "son" while, on the other hand, in France a person called "Mac" may attract notice in polite academic and analytic circles since this is the abbreviated form of *maquereau* (pimp). Although the two Macs are unrelated, they cannot be kept apart. Of course, not all of McLuhan's French readers participated in this renaming game or, for that matter, name-calling game. McLuhan and MacLuhan would appear alongside each other in contributions to learned journals and newspapers; French translations of books written by McLuhan became, under review, books by MacLuhan.

There were readers and commentators, however, whose desire had an object and appeared to them in this object: the little *a* of Mac. The *a* really depends upon desire. In this *a*, certain readers could identify themselves, even though this little sliver of a broken mirror might very well disappear in the next version of McLuhan's name. For a reader whose desire is tied to this object and whose subjecthood is constituted by it, this instability is doubly significant, since it indicates the fragility of this constitution and the division of the desiring subject who accomplishes it. In other words, McLuhan needs to be constantly rewritten as MacLuhan so as to embody the object of fantasy of the desiring subject. Yet no amount of constitutive respelling can change the significance of the little *a* as an image in which the subject's lack appears to him/her.

I am supposing that the little *a* is akin to an *objet petit a*. There are limits to this Lacanian supposition as a strategy of making sense of a cultural phenomenon since, as the deconstructionist reader of psychoanalysis Mikkel Borch-Jacobsen (1991) reminds us, the *objet a* is a part of oneself which one separates from oneself: a quite literal – that is, real – matter of giving up or sacrificing a bodily substance or organ, the loss of which is irrecuperable. But it is also imaginary. The little *a* of Mac is not a real body part. Bertolt Brecht's gangster Macheath – "Mac the Knife" from *The Threepenny Opera* – has neither turned his blade on himself nor on the other, although in principle he handles a knife as well as or better than Macbeth. Still, the little *a* of Mac is a typographic morsel dropped into the gap between *M* and *c*, which it moreover manifests as it drops into place, as one would expect of an *objet petit a* since it is a "symbol of the lack . . . in so far as it is lacking" (Lacan 1977a: 103).

I am not chasing after spittle, sperm, feces, the maternal breast, Van Gogh's ear, etc.: these real objects which a body separates from itself or "sacrifices," as it were. The diversity of such objects requires a typology distinguishing, for example, those that are cut and those from which one is weaned; Lacan's "unthinkable list" (1977b: 315) indicates just how hard it is to put one's finger on the *objet petit a*; another list, no less thinkable, includes breasts, feces, the gaze and the voice (Lacan 1977a: 242). All the same, the little *a* is figurally a "little pile," an abject loop with a tail, a curled dropping evacuated from a pen, perhaps even a compositorial trace.

What's in a name? The *a* of Mac circulates in and out of a family name. It is a fiction that embodies desire. This *objet petit a* slips in and out of signification through the passageway between *M* and *c* despite the well-known claim that it "falls outside of signification" by "evading the signifier" (Grigg 1991: 112; and "resists significantization" in Borch-Jacobsen 1991). It plays the game of presence/absence better than other signifiers because it comes and goes as the reader/writer pleases. It is less a matter of resistance than one of unpredictability and at times fickleness (it's a bit like television, I suppose: there isn't much on when it's on, and for some, there's not much going on when it's off). The little *a* holds the prophet and his disciples together and it is a letter that has had and continues to have a hold on the French imagination. In Alfred Jarry's (1972) "neoscientific novel" *Gestes et opinions du Docteur Faustroll*, the doctor's assistant Bosse-de-Nage utters two French words at opportune moments throughout the text: "Ha Ha." Baudrillard (1976) understands this laughter in terms of the formula "A = A," the operational and tautological perfection of a system grown as obese as a *gidouille*, and therefore ready to be pushed over the edge by means of the revolutionary pataphysical principle of "more A than A." A string of identical little mathemes (aaaaa . . .) is a laughable object (see Genosko 1994). It is only a matter of time and, indeed, alphabetic inevitability, that *objets b* and *c* come into existence as residuality proliferates like television channels.

MACK

McLuhan began his correspondence with the British painter, writer and polemicist (less kindly, for many, a fascist) Wyndham Lewis in the early 1940s from his post at St. Louis University. During this period Lewis was teaching at Assumption College in Windsor, Ontario. McLuhan vigorously promoted Lewis as a portrait artist and had some success in opening the "big pocket-books," as he called them, of St. Louis. McLuhan also arranged lectures for Lewis. The nickname "Mac" was adopted by McLuhan himself as a short form in a letter to Lewis in 1944 (McLuhan 1987: 142–43). For years thereafter McLuhan signed his letters to Lewis with "Mac." According to the editors of McLuhan's published *Letters*, Lewis remarked upon this nickname to the effect that "Mack is not too matey, but it is too generic. I have known so many 'Macks' – it blurs the image. Shall think up a less dignified abbreviation of my *Feldherr*" (McLuhan 1987: 142, n. 1). This "Mac attack" did not in the end deter McLuhan, although Lewis appears to have used it sparingly. Meanwhile, McLuhan adopted it as his moniker with several other correspondents. Lewis himself blurred the image with the addition of the final *k*, suggesting another big American object, a truck. The nickname or *Surnommant* of Lewis's *Feldherr* opens onto the matter of the remainder central to the *objet a*. By overnaming his *Feldherr* Mac, a diminished name actually and ironically accomplished the production of a surplus. There is something special, then, about the *k*. Along similar lines, Eugene Holland (1988) signified the Americanization of Lacan's theories through the bastard eponym Lackanianism.

McLuhan ultimately admitted in a letter of January 1944 that "'McLuhan' suits me and is preferable to 'mac'" (1987: 146). Indeed, for a field marshal patroling the promotional front, "Mac" was simply and sardonically too dignified and indistinct for Lewis's taste. Despite this, Lewis never came up with a new name. And while he had doubts about his little name, McLuhan continued to use it in his correspondence with one of his former graduate students in St. Louis, Walter J. Ong, as well as with his colleague Felix Giovanelli. Ezra Pound put his own twist on McLuhan with "Mc L," a subtle architectural arrangement which had little of the chuminess of Lewis's remarks, but sufficient ideographic peculiarity to amuse them both (McLuhan 1987: 232, nn. 3, 4). This is, then, the story of Mac before it was taken up by McLuhan's French readers in the 1960s, having long since disappeared from view in McLuhan's correspondence with Lewis. In the manner of Lewis's (1981a, 1981b) Vorticist journals *BLAST* 1 (orig. June 1914) and *BLAST* 2 (orig. July 1915), whose influence on McLuhan would be decisive in the areas of book design and rhetorical posturing, one might say:

> Blast Mack for its British chuminess;
> Bless Mac for its Gallic mannerism.

Lacan and McLuhan come together through the letter-object *a* rather than under the glare of the video's light, that records, for some, the meetings of great men. Lacan was a master of the media, not the absolute master, of course, since this position was reserved for McLuhan. Consider Sherry Turkle's (1981: 201–2) description of Lacan with reference to the broadcast of an interview with him called *Psychoanalysis* in January 1973 (published as *Télévision* the following year) by the ORTF:

> Lacan established himself as the undisputed master of the media, or as one analyst, who has always been hostile to Lacan but who said he was "overwhelmed by a virtuoso performance," described him: "The psychoanalyst for the Age of McLuhan." Like a neurotic's symptom, Lacan's *Télévision* was a program that people loved to hate.

French television viewers had already entered *la galaxie MacLuhan* during his appearance *au petit écran* on July 5, 1972 as part of the program *"Dossiers de l'écran"* (one needs to keep in mind that this was before Bernard Pivot and "Apostrophes"; see Heath 1989). McLuhan's appearance was organized by the telecommunications engineer and music professor Pierre Schaeffer, long-serving Chef du service de la RTF (and later ORTF). In the early 1970s, Schaeffer was one of McLuhan's promoters in French media circles. Later in the decade, however, Schaeffer's (1978–79: 104ff.) criticisms of McLuhan's work became severe. His charges included professional and political irresponsibility, conceptual confusion, and, above all else, deception. For Schaeffer, McLuhan was the first university professor to draw positive attention to the media. McLuhan made the media a legitimate object of intellectual concern, and in doing so presented Schaeffer with the opportunity to elevate his own work and position in the eyes of the French professors for whom the media had hitherto remained below their lofty gaze. In what Schaeffer regarded as often brilliant texts, McLuhan failed to live up to his promise of securing the study of media a place in the academy, adhering instead to jokes, bad journalistic practices and sensationalism. In short, Schaeffer claimed that McLuhan's texts were surrealistic and they distracted French researchers from developing their own lines of inquiry into the mediascape. Schaeffer did not take any blame for what he called, with as much cliché as prescience, *l'affaire McLuhan* (bringing to mind the more recent print media event, *l'affaire Derrida*), although he helped to stage McLuhan's entry into French televisual consciousness. Despite the poignancy of Schaeffer's predicament, media workers found themselves making similar statements again and again during the course of McLuhan's French revolution.

McLuhan was not particularly pleased with his performance(s) on French television. He wrote to his friends Tom and Dorothy Easterbrook that they "were complicated by my inadequate French." Still, Paris provided Mac with the pleasing diversion of Eugène Ionesco's play *MacBett*, performed for the first time at Le Théâtre Rive-Gauche in 1972 (*MP* 23/19). For its part, television provided McLuhan with a low-definition rendezvous with the French public, a doubly cool (owing to the medium and the messenger) point of contact deepened by his awkward oral skills which would have necessitated, for those who cared to listen, a high level of involvement in the completion and perhaps correction of his remarks. McLuhan had mastered the medium before he had mastered French. A perfectly fluent McLuhan may have been too hot for French audiences and, by the same token, a transparent and straight-forwardly descriptive Lacan could not have "mastered" television. Lacan was never cooler than on television – except, perhaps, when he was thought to be addressing a dog while standing on a soapbox during a talk at Vincennes (Lacan 1990: 117).

It is evident from letters written to his family from Cambridge in the 1930s that the French language and culture had entered McLuhan's consciousness in an enthusiastic but incomplete manner. These letters radiate youthful exuberance and his belief that the mastery of French opens one to "the mind of the greatest European people" (1987: 28). While McLuhan did become a competent reader of French, he later lamented that he read only this language in addition to his own. Unlike his friend Lewis (1981a: 13), McLuhan would not "Blast Parisian Parochialism" and "Sentimental Gallic Gush."

MA – MA – MA – MA

The journalist Guy Dumur reported on his meeting with McLuhan at the ORTF and the prophet's television appearance(s) for readers of *La Nouvel Observateur* shortly after "*Dossiers de l'écran*" was aired. McLuhan was a media personality and therefore newsworthy in the eyes of the media, turned as they are toward themselves. Dumur claimed ignorance when it came to evaluating

McLuhan's intellectual contributions. Despite what McLuhan's admirers such as Schaeffer, Morin, Jean Duvignaud and Alain Bourdin have claimed in the name of an "open" sociology, Dumur (1972: 36–37) simply could not understand McLuhan because "he is too Anglo-Saxon" (this was a rather odd thing to say of a Celt). Nevertheless, it was already commonplace in journalistic reports on McLuhan to claim that his work was contrary to the French spirit of Cartesian thought. Figured as an "anti-Descartes," McLuhan challenged the methods of separation, dissection and causal explanation by stringing together apparently unrelated ideas; this latter practice made his texts surrealistic, and surrealism had long since passed out of fashion.

But for many French journalists, several pieces of the puzzle of McLuhan always seemed to be missing. More to the point, Daniel Garric and others specified that while English is direct, and permits the formation of neologisms and explosive links between disparate ideas, French is at the pole opposite of *la pensée McLuhanienne* because it is intimately neo-classical in construction (Garric 1967a, 1967b; Marcotte 1974). This rather sweeping claim helped to fuel the charge that he was difficult to understand in translation, which was quite true at one level, but had little to do with the formation of neologisms.

These vague contrasts set the stage for more bizarre pronouncements, themselves worthy of the label "surreal." For example, Dominique Desanti (1974: 40–41) referred mistakenly to McLuhan as "un pur WASP!" White – yes – but Anglo-Saxon and Protestant – no; well, at least not after his conversion to Catholicism. Moreover, a mantra was being chanted in Parisian circles courtesy, among others, of the journalist associated with *Le Figaro Littéraire*, André Brincourt (1972): "Ma – Ma – Ma – Ma: Marx, Mao, Marshall McLuhan." The last syllable of the chant indicated what it was in the prophet and so-called revolutionary that was more than himself, an *objet petit a* that did not in this instance find its way into his name, but nonetheless transfixed those like Brincourt sunk in their chanting; it may as well have been Macheath, MacBett, Macbeth, MacDonalds, MacLuhan (whom, it is rumored, enjoyed more than a few Big Macs in his time). One needn't go further than Yves Knockaert's (1988) *Third Interlude* for piano to find a soundtrack suitable for Big Mac's periodic Mac Attacks; after all, he composed this piece for a ballet aptly titled *MacLuhan at MacDonalds*. What is also more than itself or the residue of the residue of the name? It is the further remainder that reminds us of a cry for mother: mama, mama. The pain of this cry is real enough because it wants satisfaction from an object from which one will soon enough be weaned. This *objet petit a* belongs to the (m)other or ma-ma.

Writing in the introduction to Jean Marabini's (1973) book *Marcuse & McLuhan et la nouvelle révolution mondiale*, Armand Lanoux refers to "les deux grands M: M et M," whose respective revolutionary ideas are said to be like thermometers, since it is absurd to blame them for the heat they register.

Lanoux's activities in the French media included his presidency of the Comité de la télévision française in the late 1950s, as well as the directorship of the review À *la page* from 1964 to 1970. Today, the very notion that Marx, Mao, Marcuse and MacLuhan could be brought together in a consciousness-raising chant about youth and revolution indicates the brilliant superficiality of mediatic representations of the political field and the abuses of "Eastern" practices prevalent in the 1960s. Several years before Marabini's book and, writing in Montréal, Renault Gariépy (1967) had observed in the heady atmosphere of Expo '67 that "on our little French screen . . . the presence of MM (these initials no longer translate the reality of Marilyn Monroe or Mickey Mantle) has begun to make itself felt." A Canadian "MM" had temporarily eclipsed – no mean feat – several American standards. Let's not forget that years after "MM" disappeared from the French scene, another MM (Mickey Mouse), a further American standard, would make his presence felt.

The little *a* is the remainder, the surplus of the prophet's message. This message was a sublime object of fascination inspiring an impressive range of responses. McLuhan's flaws (his awkward French, his alleged journalistic excesses, flippancy, political irresponsibility in the eyes of the Left) helped to solidify his position as prophet rather than diminish his status. As Slavoj Žižek (1991: 254–55) explains in the case of the body of the king, his ordinary features undergo a transubstantiation as he becomes an object of fascination. To debase the king is not to diminish his status, since the accentuation of his flaws reinforces his position by arousing compassion and fascination. This holds equally true in the case of the prophet MacLuhan, especially in his heyday. The more his work was subjected to critical debate, the more fascinating he became. A sublime object is a difficult target to hit, for the *objet petit a* is a second-order semblance framed by a television screen. Having smashed the set, the medium may reassert itself through the adjoining wall of a neighbor's apartment, in a bar, in a picture window of a shop, etc. Standing over the wreck of a television set or, to use Žižek's example, over the body of Ceaușescu, one asks oneself: is it/he really dead? The *objet petit a* cannot be destroyed – unlike one of the sign vehicles by means of which it is temporarily delivered – and this is brought home by the image of Ceaușescu's body broadcast televisually around the world, persisting not only in the memory of Romanians but in the international image banks. The lost *objet a* needs a medium to clothe it; even a name will suffice. Of course, MacLuhan was not subject to the regicidal intentions of his televisual audience. This did not make him any easier to hit. For the paradox of striking MacLuhan was this: it put one in the strange position of being seen as a counter-revolutionary, for one was thought to be on the side of mechanical reason and rationality, Western values, on the wrong side of the "generation gap," anti-youth, a proponent of explication over exploration. In short, because MacLuhan aligned himself with youth culture and counter-cultural revolution against the academy, to attack him as a counter-revolutionary was paradoxically to become one oneself (see Dommergues 1969). Ultimately, however, MacLuhan's own corporatist assumptions, homophobia, and "right to life" politics were read as the signs of a deeply conservative Catholic thinker. No paradox could, in the end, erase or obscure these beliefs.

The little *a* embodies the impossible *jouissance* of certain members of the French media community, such as Schaeffer. The realization that their prophet was also an impostor caught them in a painful paradox. Mac could not provide "it"; that is, he could not satisfy the desire of media workers for legitimation in relation to the French intellectuals. As he continued not to provide "it," Mac still embodied the *objet a* of the legitimation fantasy as it showed those such as Schaeffer what they were: little twisted semblances of shit. Even the message of the medium, critically battered, taught a painful lesson about exclusion from intellectual discourse, while at the same time it filled page after page of reviews: Yes, it's all over with Mac, isn't it? It was his success that destroyed him, wasn't it? We technicians must have been wrong. It needs to be said again, doesn't it? This was the rather lengthy lesson taught by the little *a* of Mac. But Mac was not an analyst – although, as we saw earlier with respect to the concept of rationalization, he sometimes was figured as one – who could teach his followers how to give up the *objet petit a* and readjust themselves to French intellectual life in the wake of another failed revolution; to give his name back its quasi-original spelling, leaving a gap between *M* and *c* which would really show the technicians where they belonged and of what they were made.

There is nothing particularly original in this situation. In the 1960s, *les moyens de masse* in France were often the concern of para-academic media workers or cultural *animateurs*. A further example is found in Brian Rigby's analysis of the *Vivre son temps* collection of books published from 1962 to 1967, and edited by Jacques Charpentreau. "All the writers in the collection agreed," Rigby writes (1991: 44), "that the new phenomenon facing France in the early to mid-1960s was that of *mass* society." Few of these writers had university posts. They were *animateurs* committed to bringing high culture to the masses. They sought to humanize new technologies and play a mediating role in the "permanent education" of the masses. While Rigby treats these writers as intellectuals, he notes:

> In the eyes of some French academics and intellectuals, this group of writers may well not seem very distinguished. One can even image sociologists such as Bourdieu and his disciples refusing to acknowledge that they were part of an authentic intelligentsia.
>
> (Rigby 1991: 44)

The division between cultural action and the scholarly field or, to use other terms, between the cultural *animateurs* and intellectuals-academics, was played out in *l'affaire McLuhan*. Rigby's imagination did not need very much exercise to evoke the class politics of the study of the mass media in France in the 1960s. McLuhan was perceived as inauthentic by the intellectuals because of the support of the *animateurs* and his interest in their work; the *animateurs* considered his work authentic precisely because he appealed to their practices from the site of the academy and the television studio and could be said to have recognized something to which French intellectuals had hitherto been blind. The *animateurs* are a little like desire since they are never content (to let the masses pursue their own delirious ends in the mediascape).

One of the most important features of McLuhan's reception in France was the issue of who read and promoted him and the sites from which they worked. While those in the mass media, artists of all stripes, especially graphic artists, and pedagogues eager to introduce new audio-visual tools into the classroom, found inspiration in his theories, this led to claims that it was his success that destroyed him, and that the prestige accorded him did not originate from a legitimate site.

With the advent of the concept of *macluhanisme* there emerged the figure of a prophet who might have provided satisfaction for the "[wo]men of images," the professionals of the communications industries (advertisers, media technicians, printers, designers and teachers). But the prophet failed to do so, as we have seen, for several reasons; and with this disappointment came a barrage of criticism against him. The very inseparability of the desire of the "[wo]men of images" and the object-cause of their desire led to very public suffering and loss of potential prestige and glory.

François Mariet (1978–79: 108–9) correctly diagnosed this situation in recognizing that *macluhanisme* "is inseparable from the public whose expectations it fulfills and for whom McLuhan becomes . . . a prophet." Occupying a position subordinate to the theoretical disciplines of the academy from which concepts are borrowed, and less well known than philosophers, writers and filmmakers, the media workers, represented by Mariet as a "fan club," entered the public sphere of intellectual debate only to have their own subordinate position displayed to them in the media in which they worked. Moreover, in his study of the recognition factor of *macluhanisme* among teachers in France, Mariet cataloged the diverse effects of hearsay and found that McLuhan's French readers in the pedagogical milieu needed no specific competence in order to tune into his messages. This made him enormously popular. Mariet (1977: 51) attributes the success of *macluhanisme* among teachers to the "conjunction of this diffuse expectation of a philosophy of the media and to an unusual oeuvre in which no scientific method of demonstration limits the access of the hurried or untrained reader, and against which no critical text forewarns." Mariet situates himself on the side of the critical, unhurried pedagogue, the trained reader who specializes in identifying the follies of interpretation of a servile class.

On the other hand of this rhetoric of speed, the hurried McReader has no time to reflect, Mariet suggests. But among such typographically minded groups as the Association des Campagnons de Lure, for example, points of resistance against just this sort of professional pronouncement had been established in the course of a seminar (attended by McLuhan in August 1969) devoted to "M. McL." In his introduction to the seminar, Gilles Gheerbrand (1969) presents a reading of three categories of French articles on McLuhan (reviews; those that purport to reveal the fraud of *macluhanisme*; and serious and honest reflections), the second of which briefly describes some of the errors made by the intellectuals in their attempts to discredit McLuhan, while hinting at the similarity of some of their ideas to those of McLuhan. Even distinguished university professor François Châtelet, Gheerbrand remarks, read McLuhan hurriedly, pointing out his error of thinking that the telephone was a hot medium. The speed of one's reading was the shit that was flung back and forth over the course of the public debates on the merits of McLuhan. How did McLuhan himself read? He was not a slow and careful hermeneut by any stretch of the imagination. His reading habits were, as biographer Philip Marchand (1989: 129) explains, selective:

> To determine whether a book was worth reading, he usually looked at page 69 of the work, plus the adjacent page and the table of contents. If the author gave no promise of insight or worthwhile information on page 69, McLuhan reasoned, the book was probably not worth reading. If he decided the book did merit his attention, he started by reading only the left hand pages.

The charge of unreflective speed reading could not be used effectively against McLuhan's followers on the grounds of its inadequacy to the master's habits and the texts they informed. One may claim against his detractors that the errors of their readings were the result of slow reading against the grain.

Into the gap between desire and fulfillment went the little *a* of Mac, and the prophet was taken as the cause of his subjects' desires. *Le mac* or the pimp didn't and couldn't deliver; or rather, he delivered his followers into servitude. This does not mean that they went without a struggle. Žižek would have us believe that such servitude is voluntary since the other name, the sublime Mac, hypnotized his readers because they conferred upon it the power to do so. They were glued to their sets, if you will; and, after smashing them, they were glued to the idea of the set that Mac preached. To be called *un petit mac* carries a further meaning. *Un mac* is a person who invites a guest to dinner and, when the time comes to settle the bill, notices that he is short of money, and asks his guest for a loan. Mac's followers suffered the indignity of having to pay the price of accepting an invitation to bring their work to the intellectual table, a table set for them in the name of their host, but for which they had to pay dearly, and pay some more.

Both "*le pape du pop*," as Garric once dubbed McLuhan in a Catholic gesture (in this name alone one senses why the dictates of the prophet were followed to the letter by certain believers), and Lacan renounced personal brilliance in the name of orders greater than themselves; for Lacan, it was sainthood. The saintly psychoanalyst, too, embodies the *objet petit a* and it is one of the "oddities of the acts of saints," Lacan noted (1990: 15–16), to make those whose ears were glued to their television sets aware of this and to unstick them. It was only after the program was over, after the blue glow of the screen had dissipated, and Lacan was silent – as mum as a saint – that one could really hear what one is in the sound of sight. The important displacement hinted at by Lacan is that of sight by sound, eye by ear, even before the television set. Recall, however, that we are in the "Age of McLuhan." This displacement was, McLuhan claimed, at the center of the Gutenberg civilization's deafening of the tribal ear for the sake of the biases of literacy and visual culture. This made one ill-equipped to experience the auditory-tactile world of the new electronic technologies. For McLuhan, tuning in meant keeping one's ears glued to the set. Unlike the saintly analyst, and despite his renunciation of personal brilliance, McLuhan didn't stop producing euphoria. He simply could not be mum in the oral-aural electronic village even if, in French, he occasionally stumbled. Watching television made *théorie à la con* – lousy theory.

4

MASSAGE AND SEMIURGY

Sémiurgie (semiurgy) is a French neologism that came into use in the early 1970s in discourses concerned with mass-mediated environments. Part sign (semi[o]-) and part work (-urgy), the concept often appears today alongside other identifying features of postmodernity, especially its purported depthlessness and nihilism. Although numerous scholars trace its lineage to Baudrillard who, for his part, seems to have modeled it on McLuhan's concept of massage, this line of descent has been uncritically accepted and insufficiently analyzed.

I will rethink this lineage by considering the important differences between Baudrillard and McLuhan as they concern semiurgy. Indeed, Baudrillard was not the only thinker for whom semiurgy had descriptive valency. The Swiss esthetician and communications theorist René Berger – in whose work some believe the term semiurgy first appeared – developed the concept along a line that diverged sharply from Baudrillard's work and converged instead with that of McLuhan.

PANIC SEMIURGY

For some postmodernists, semiurgy alone is not enough; it must be radicalized by an act of adjectival one-upmanship whose effect on the concept is pejorative. According to Kroker and Cook in *The Postmodern Scene* (1986: 24), sexuality has died two deaths. They attribute the first – a murder – to Michel Foucault, on whose hands no blood remained after he announced that our experience of natural sex with secretions was mediated by a discursive sexuality. The second – an unnatural or, rather, sociological death – saw discursive sexuality pass away due to an irreversible and incurable postmodern condition. Henceforth, sexuality will be experienced "as an endless semiurgy of signs: *panic sex*." Panic is the psychological mood of postmodernity understood semiurgically.

Sex, then, is dead; secretions are simulated, seduction is liquidated, bodies are designed products. Sexuality is experienced through technological and mediatic representations as sign play. It is not only sexuality that is dead. If Foucault murdered natural sex, and Calvin Klein killed discursive sexuality, it is left to Baudrillard to identify the corpse of experience as such. Kroker and Cook attribute the concept of "radical semiurgy" to Baudrillard. They derive several rather extreme consequences from this concept: there is no way out of the pure sign system of postmodernity; everything is exchangeable within the system; all experience is structured relationally, just as a sign's value is determined by its place in the system from which all value issues; there will be no extra-systemic emancipation, such as a resurrection of natural reference or a vertical ascension to Being. In these terms, experience is dead precisely because one is trapped in an endless series of exchanges, in a structural relationism. This is why they claim that the prevailing cultural mood is one of panic.

A few words on panic are in order. I have pointed out elsewhere (Genosko 1994: 113) that Kroker lacks a sense of the history of the esthetic applications of the concept. No matter, though, since panic in a contemporary frame is merely another way of describing postmodernity in terms of a psychological disorder. In Jameson's (1983: 118ff.) semiotic shorthand, the perpetual present of the postmodern moment is described by the breakdown of the interdependent relationship between signifiers, leading to the loss of identity over time and, paradoxically, the intensification of experience in the present, as long as it is understood that the one whose experience is under consideration lacks an identity. "In other words," Jameson writes, "schizophrenic experience is an experience of isolated, disconnected, discontinuous material signifiers which fail to link up in a coherent sequence." Psychologically, panic is a genuine disorder understood as an acute form of anxiety. In its crisis phase panic disorder takes the form of an attack in which the familiar suddenly seems like a threat: the symptomatology includes sweating, shortness of breath, heart palpitations, unsteadiness, tingling, faintness and feelings of unreality. In short, jagged emotions and physical discomfort that are concentrated in an attack, which then subsides. A panic syndrome is indicated by two or more attacks per month, often leading to anticipatory anxiety and related phobic behavior.

Sociologically, panic has been seen as a symptom of normal problem solving, a phenomenon of collective life not at all particular to postmodernity. Panic is an analyzable breach in the everyday, an aberration subjected to a restricted understanding with a very mechanical character: panic is a response to being overwhelmed; in short, it is an adaptive response to a stimulus, usually a tragedy of some sort. In postmodern terms, panic designates the extreme character of everyday life. Panic is not limited to an aberration in an adaptive economy; rather, it is a general condition, the form of life; life is overwhelming, an emergency. Panic is, for Kroker and others, assimilated to life. It's not an irrational breach but synonymous with contemporary life lived as a catastrophe in the ruins of the end of the century. Hence, this generalization allows Kroker to apply panic to just about anything. Panic lacks specificity and shape: it is one long attack in the perpetual present, a continuous emergency. In the *Panic Encyclopedia* (Kroker *et al.* 1989) the alphabet serves as a delivery mechanism for the "key psychological mood of postmodern culture." It is a device that covers a lot of bases, in other words, and provides a ready-made organization around letters; Kroker calls the entries a collection of "post-facts" or non-empirical descriptions, little factionalized sketches of events and things that come and go in a flash. This encyclopedia is without doubt a challenge to conservative programs for cultural literacy (Fogel 1989–90).

Kroker and Cook advise their readers to turn to Baudrillard's first book *Le système des objets* (1968) for an account of "radical semiurgy" in relation to the practice of consumption. Although Baudrillard does not use the term in this book, this is surely beside the point for Kroker and Cook. For the semiurgic manipulation of signs irreparably severed from their referents is akin to consumption understood as an "activity involving the systematic manipulation of signs," as Baudrillard defined it. Signs are consumed in virtue of their abstract and systematic differences with other signs as opposed to their materiality. For example, "functionality," Baudrillard argues, is an abstract system of manipulable signs interpolated between the materiality of objects and the materiality of needs. This is "meta-functional" to the extent that an object has "become an element of play, combination and calculus in a universal system of signs" (Baudrillard 1968: 77). But for Kroker and Cook, it is not only consumption that is semiurgical since experience is subjected to the combinatorial possibilities of the code of the sign system.

Charles Levin similarly explains this death of experience in the semiurgical manipulation of signs in terms of the loss of personal significance resulting from an advanced kind of fetishism in which "objects have become increasingly closed off from human interaction in their systematic self-referential play." This fetishism of the system as opposed to individual objects impoverishes and ultimately prevents meaningful social communication, since "the semiurgy of social objects reduces the availability of things for mediating social relations . . . and assigns them to mediating systems of signs instead" (Levin 1984: 42). The relations between objects are no longer lived; such structural relations have become exterior to lived situations. The abolition of real, concrete, personal and conflictual differences between persons with the homogenization of products and persons allows for the emergence of the cult of differentiation. Differences are industrially produced for the mass consumer market. The consumption of differences involves a strategy of personalization requiring affiliation with an abstract model of combinatory possibilities constituting, for instance, a fashionable "look" or adherence to a model of masculinity in which one can exclaim "he can't be a man 'cause he doesn't smoke the same cigarettes as me."

The trajectory of Baudrillard's thought over the last 30 years has been away from an analysis of objects in terms of systems and structures toward objects as destiny, as pure signs or crystals; the latter are fundamentally enigmatic and inaccessible to the subject's knowledge, to whom they are indifferent. The reversal – one of Baudrillard's key rhetorical figures – of the subject orientation to the object orientation has a rich tradition to draw upon from theater and literature (Genosko 1994: 135ff.). But analyses of objects have a tendency to reveal a peculiar movement toward the object pole, and Baudrillard (1987: 12–13) has acknowledged the influence of Barthes's description, suggesting the growing insignificance of the scene and the emergence of the interactive screen, of automobile design, specifically the Citroën. The tendency at issue here is the passage from the car as the prize possession to be projected upon and fantasized about – the "little deuce coupe" – to the car as a sanctuary, a partner coordinating the exploration of various vectors in an "uninterrupted interface," what Baudrillard calls, abandoning the imagery of speed, triumph and phallic representation, an ecology of driving.

Douglas Kellner also picks up the concept of "radical semiurgy" in his critique of Baudrillard. He defines it in general Baudrillardian terms: "*Radical semiurgy*, the production and proliferation of signs, has created a society of *simulations* governed by *hyperreality*: images, spectacles, simulations proliferate and terrorize, fascinate, and mesmerize" (Kellner 1987: 127–28). In particular, however, the "Satan of radical semiurgy" – which is Kellner's name for Baudrillard's so-called "demiurge of postmodernity" – is television. For Kellner, Baudrillard aligns semiurgy with a series of deaths (of the social, use-value, Marxism, political economy, class, feminism, etc.). What does television kill? This semiurge, a master artificer whose relationship with the demiurgic invention of evil is made explicit by Kellner, collapses critical distinctions, exhausts meaning, volatilizes reference, and blocks communication by simulating it as a response already integrated into the system – among other things. In these terms semiurgy is not only reductive but evil. It will follow for Kellner that television is also evil, and since McLuhan developed a defense of television, in courting an evil medium, he was contaminated. Television is the brush that Kellner uses to try to paint his opponents into a critical corner.

Despite their differences on many other points, Kroker and Cook, and Kellner agree that semiurgy is a key term in the "Baudrillard Scene." Moreover, they trace this concept from Baudrillard's theorizing to the work of McLuhan. The closing of the "eye of the flesh," first theorized by St. Augustine and much later painted by Magritte as a disembodied eye, Kroker and Cook claim, symbolizes the exteriorization of the human senses in postmodern experience. The disembodied eye turns experience inside out by trapping the body in a closed loop in which it becomes a servomechanism controlled by a digital logic and activated by media technologies. The inner relational structure of this narcissian loop is semiurgical. Kroker and Cook note that

> Baudrillard's theorization of the "radical semiurgy" at work in the imposition of an "image-system" as the structure of social exchange is very similar to McLuhan's conception of the "massaging" of the ratio of the senses in a cybernetic society.
>
> (Kroker and Cook 1986: 298, n. 17)

Technological extensions of human faculties (psychic or physical) demand "new sense ratios," among other extensions, as McLuhan argued in *Understanding Media* and *The Medium Is the Massage*. Media work over the body completely, massaging it as it were, by intensifying certain faculties, diminishing others, and establishing new proportions between them. The term "servomechanism" was used by McLuhan to describe how one relates to technologies, that is, how one narcissistically serves extensions of oneself.

McLuhan used the Narcissus myth to indicate that the beautiful youth Narcissus did not fall in love with himself, as the myth is commonly read. Rather, Narcissus fell in love with a technological extension of himself. While McLuhan recognized Narcissus's narcotic autoeroticism in relation to the nymph Echo's spurned love, he believed the youth's loss of his ability to communicate sexually may be nonetheless reparable. The thin film of water which kept Narcissus apart from his double no longer interferes with the New Narcissus's sexual relations with extensions of himself. As Donald Theall (1971: 124) has observed, the New Narcissus "fecundates his images, the technology that he has generated and that is changing him." Despite this recognition of mechanical sexual relations, Theall notes that the massage is never fully mutual because McLuhan was more interested in how one is massaged by the media, each of which has specialties that produce internal and external changes in oneself.

Kellner, too, has linked Baudrillardian semiurgy to McLuhan's focus on the form of the media, and he uses the concept of "media semiurgy" to describe the multiple collapses toward entropy of the means by which critical distinctions are made and maintained. The media demiurge fashions new social relations and experiences out of signs freed from their concepts and referents. Kellner decries any capitulation to the power of televisual semiurgy.

Understood semiurgically, massage is unilateral and the New Narcissus will at best have to simulate a countermassage. Kroker and Cook (1986: 198, n. 17) credit Fekete (1982) with a "superb account of the semiurgical process in McLuhan's thought." But Fekete's generous explication is Baudrillardian; this is certainly a far cry from his earlier comprehensive Marxist critique of McLuhan as a counterrevolutionary — "the major bourgeois ideologue of the one-dimensional society" (1973: 121). Baudrillard's claims concerning the media's fabrication of non-communication and the prevention of response are used by Fekete (1982: 57–58) to demonstrate the analytic value of McLuhan's polysemic sense of massage. Semiurgy and massage both designate powerful forces reshaping social experience. As mass processes, they are similar; but the effects of this processing of the masses are quite different.

Baudrillardian semiurgy is a disruptive force which traps, breaks, collapses, reduces and simulates experience and communication; it is alienating. Technological massage also can be numbing, exhausting and bewildering, and requires protective ablations. McLuhan believed that this numbing fades over time as sensitivity and awareness are regained. New shifts in sense ratios require certain perceptual displacements which are stressful, and a new sensory equilibrium results from these shifts. Understood physiologically, massage stimulates circulation; and it is supposedly emancipatory with respect to social communication, as McLuhan insisted in his description of the involvement demanded by electronic environments. Semiurgy is, however, finally involved with itself and the relations of a closed system.

In the Canadian context, the relationship between McLuhan and Baudrillard has been underlined in the work of Kroker. Kroker's own intellectual development has become the occasion for the fusion of business, performance and postmodern theory, very much in the manner of McLuhan in his prime.

In the *Canadian Journal of Political and Social Theory* (*CJPST*) of the early 1980s, Kroker's articles (1980, 1981, 1982a) were inspired by critical theory and flavored with dashes of Foucault and even the Left liberalism of PET (Trudeau). With a significant article exposing Augustine to the winds of contemporary French sociological theory (1982b), we are introduced to a wild Augustine and an ecumenical textual practice. Lyotard (1984) would also make a similar "foundational" claim for Augustine, but in relation to modernity rather than postmodernity. By the time this essay resurfaced in Kroker and David Cook's (1986) vision of "excremental culture," there was no doubt that Augustine was the first link in the "great chain of nihilation" leading up to Baudrillard. If the classicist Charles Norris Cochrane made Augustine dangerous again, and Baudrillard made Marx dangerous once more (Kroker 1985), then it would be difficult to deny that it was Baudrillard who made Kroker dangerous. Where's Marx? He doesn't come into his own until Baudrillard teases out the Nietzsche in him. Kroker does not so much read *Capital* as reposition it in his genealogical chain of Western nihilism. "Dangerous" seems to signify both the renewal of the ability to intervene critically and the adoption of a manner, an attitude which jeopardizes this ability by dissolving into posturing, no matter how ironic it may understand itself to be. Where's McLuhan? Despite his affiliations with Baudrillard and, even more importantly, his place in the Catholic humanist tradition, McLuhan did not cut a nihilistic figure. The figure of McLuhan in Kroker's writings anticipates his more recent adoption as a patron saint of new media technologies.

Kroker rode out a wave of his own generation, like a wave machine in a postmodern mall, onto the beachhead of Baudrillard's challenges by means of calculated mimetic extensions of the "multiple refusals" of the social, the subject and emancipatory politics. The final refusal understood as an extension was to refuse Baudrillard himself:

> [his] insight in *Simulations* that the "real is that of which it is possible to give an equivalent re-production" is now rendered obsolescent by the actual transformations of the simulacrum with its hyperreality effects into its opposite: a *virtual* technology mediated with designer bodies processed through computerized imaging-systems. When technology in its ultramodernist phase connects again with the primitivism of mythic fear turned radical, it's no longer the Baudrillardian world of the simulacrum and hyperrealism, but a whole new scene of *virtual* technology and the end of the fantasy of the real.
>
> (Kroker and Cook 1986:15)

While in this mature nihilism we are "bored but hyper" or, as Steven Maras (1989: 174) puts it, this Warholian witticism "can also mean that we're hyper but bored." Kroker and Cook ask us to "forget Baudrillard" and move into a "postmodern primitivism." The vehicle of this movement is none other than the "potlatch gone postmodern," a souped-up version of Baudrillard's lost referent of symbolic exchange. It's a high-tech potlatch of global proportions: McLuhan-inspired electric tribalism based upon interiorization rather than exteriorization. Kroker's McLuhanism is most evident in his technological determinism. Virtuality contributes to a vision of an *a*semiological wave, a postsymbolic splash, to tamper with Kroker's (1984) description of McLuhan's attempt to humanize a technological field that washes over human beings. Baudrillard lights the way for Kroker's journey from McLuhan – a massage to an open-handed slap, from wave to tsunami – to a "tribal" virtuality. In Kroker's *Technology and the Canadian Mind: Innis/McLuhan/Grant* (1984), George Grant is ground to McLuhan's figure. Using the trajectory of this study as a way of situating Kroker, one begins with the "technological dependency" of Grant, advances to the "technological humanism" of McLuhan, graduates to the "technological realism" of Harold Innis, wallows in the "technological hyperrealism" of Baudrillard, and soars into the "technological virtuality" of Kroker. Here, Baudrillard is figure to McLuhan's ground and Baudrillard is ground to Kroker's figure.

SIGNWORK

None of the aforementioned critics has focussed on Baudrillard's specific use of "semiurgy." The concept comes into play in his essay "Design et environnement ou l'escalade de l'économie politique" in *Pour une critique de l'économie politique du signe* (1972). Indeed, the English translation of this essay heightens the sense of the semiurgical processing of human experience by rendering the consequent terms of the disjunction as "How Political Economy Escalates into Cyberblitz" (Baudrillard 1981a: 185). *Metallurgic* or industrial society has mutated, Baudrillard writes, into a *semiurgic* society, a techno-culture or post-industrial society. During this mutation products have become objects and objects have become forms. For Baudrillard, objects are neither things nor categories. An object is a form that is neither determined specifically by the forms of the commodity nor the Saussurean sign; indeed, an object's status is not determined in relation to a subject; neither is it established by its use as an implement by means of which things in the world are worked upon. Work in metals has given way to the work of signs.

An object, then, "is a status of meaning and a form" which is determined by its interdependent and oppositional relations with other objects. In short, an object's value is determined by the system in which it inheres. In Baudrillard's analysis, the system in question is the design theory of the Bauhaus school, which admits of coded combinatorial possibilities following from the dictate that "there is for every form and every object a determinate *signified* – its function" (Baudrillard 1972: 244–45). Baudrillard traces, in fact, the birth of the system of objects to the Bauhaus: "It is the Bauhaus that institutes this universal semantization of the environment in which everything becomes an object of a functional calculus and signification. Total functionality. Total semiurgy" (1972: 230). In the designed environment, everything is an object; each of its elements can be mastered and manipulated (assembled and reassembled). This operational semiology or semiurgy entails the control of participation in the environment; that is, one "participates" in the designed world by its own means and in its own terms – "in the data processing mode," as Baudrillard puts it, "by the circulation of signs and messages" (1972: 251). In other words, "participation" is simulacral because it is dictated by the combinatorial possibilities of the code. Remember that simulation was a Bauhaus specialty: objects appeared to be machine-made by the most intense handicraft-based operations.

Baudrillard has had a longstanding interest in designed environments. This is evident in the conception of ambiance he developed in *Le système des objets* (1968). The calculus of objects requires that one treats residential dwelling spaces as problems to be solved. Solutions are provided by interior designers with reference to abstract models that create, contradictorily, a personal arrangement or solution suitable to one's own taste. Atmosphere is a calculus of colors, materials, forms; that is, a calculated equilibrium of tones and rhythms far beyond the poetic, metaphoric and even visceral-subjective qualities of objects.

Baudrillard treats design as a meta-political economy of the sign seeking to stage "communication" between humans and the environment by means of a proliferation of signs and messages. This project is couched in terms of restoring or healing estranged relations, but ultimately only serves the better to align, in Baudrillard's estimation, and hold such participants in their places (in their abstract separateness) in the system so that what he believes to be "genuine" communication is structurally precluded.

Baudrillard's conclusion that the meta-political economy of design has produced a "society that *has become its own environment*" is precisely the point at which McLuhan arrived and advertised on one of his "posters" in *The McLuhan Dew-Line Newsletter*:

> The 70's will see: *A rampage of ecological legal prosecutions for disservice environments created by old "services."* This legal rampage against corporations will seem mysterious, polymorphous, perverse. In fact, it stems from the END OF NATURE, the beginning of the satellite environment. When the planet became the content of a man-made surround, it ceased to be NATURE for its occupants. It has to be programmed totally from now on. It is our *oikos*, our household.
>
> (McLuhan 1969e)

McLuhan delivered this piece of forecasting in "the exalted mode," Baudrillard laments. Ecology is, in McLuhan's terms, a service environment "beyond nature"; the planetary village is wired. This is the kind of nature Baudrillard considers to be reconstituted, like a fruit drink, as environment, by means of crystals with simulated flavors. Although in general terms Baudrillard and McLuhan may be said to share a similar understanding of environment as semiurgy and massage, Baudrillard refuses McLuhan's optimism because communication and participation in this designed universe cannot measure up to his own exalted vision of genuine communication: a reciprocal, simultaneous (immediate and unmediatized), transparent, inter-personal, incessant and agonistic exchange between persons which smashes the digital logic of the code and breaks the structure of the communication grid by injecting ambivalence (and not ambiguity) into messages.

Baudrillard was busy in the early 1970s lecturing on design to groups as diverse as the Chamber of Commerce in Reims, the Institut de l'environ-nement in Paris, and to students at Vincennes and the Ecole des hautes études commerciales. At the same time René Berger, a less well-known reader of McLuhan, was engaged in a parallel study of the semiurgical enterprise of post-industrial society at the Université de Lausanne.

In *Simuler/dissimuler*, Jacques Monnier-Raball (1979) claims that the French neologism *sémiurgique* (in its adjectival form) was coined by Berger in his book *La mutation des signes*, published the same year (1972) as Baudrillard's *Pour une critique*. Monnier-Raball himself evokes the devalued semioscape of advertising as a kind of "semiurgic frenzy [that] grips the city, like the devaluation of visual 'money' prompts the hasty issue of new notes, as so many overdrawn cheques" (1979: 12). *Pan-sémie* is another of the neologist Berger's coined terms. Although it does not directly imply the overdrawn accounts of the urban semiosphere, it is not the sort of neologism which can be met, Berger observes, with an occasional smile since it designates the everyday reality of living in an environment saturated with trademarks and, in general, with commercial signs of every description. Berger (1977: 87) would later coin the term *enseignerie* by combining the word for a shop's sign (*enseigne*) with the Gallicized term for the work of an engineer (*ingénerie*), retaining the latter's etymological link with *engin* (both instrument and ruse), in the service of designating the signs, signals and visual stimuli of the urban environment. *Pan-sémie* is a semio-cultural phenomenon corresponding to massification in industry and communications. Berger (1972: 406) thinks that the relationship between products and needs has been broken and reconfigured by the focus of needs, wishes and desires on the valorized representations of products. With this acknowledgment, Berger gestures toward a Baudrillardian political economy of the sign.

Pan-sémie operates at the speed of advanced communications technologies and thus surpasses the relatively slow and limited circuits through which cultural traditions are disseminated. Like McLuhan, Berger held that mass-mediated electric environments were poorly understood by many of those for whom such environments were commented upon critically. But speed is itself, Berger specifies, a transmitter; it "strikes the set," to use one of McLuhan's theatrical metaphors (McLuhan 1969b), of reflective humanist pedagogues (and traditional educational institutions) lagging behind a culture no longer their own. Berger (1972: 298–303) praises explicitly McLuhan's critique of arguments based upon good and bad uses of the media and the somnambulism of traditional humanists, for whom content is the object of knowledge.

Berger asks us to consider that signs are produced and these products themselves have in their turn products specific to the demiurges of public relations and advertising firms. Such signs are fabricated and targeted in the name of producing identification and consumption, and they are also "products" subject to study by semiologists. Berger asks:

> For how long a time will intellectuals accept professing to be semiologists when many manufacturers, admen and owners of mass media are already "semiurgists" making signs and imposing them on us?
>
> (Berger 1972: 21)

No science can escape this question, Berger thinks. Reflection is indissociable from action. No change can take place until this relation is understood and pseudo-objectivity, false neutrality and traditional conceptions of critical distance are called into question. Berger's key contribution to answering the question "what is semiurgy?" lies in his analysis of the relationship between semiology and semiurgy or, more generally, between "logies and/or urgies" (1972: 409).

On the one hand, "-logy" designates sciences (geology, semiology, *et alia*) in which certain phenomena (objects) are identified and incorporated into a body of knowledge. The accent is on, Berger writes, *mise en forme reglée* (imposition of a model); that is, on information, discourse and the comportment of the knowing subject in relation to its objects. On the other hand, "-urgy" signifies the *mise en oeuvre* (implementation) contained in metallurgy, demiurgy, semiurgy, *et alia*. Rather than a cognitive attitude, "-urgy" demands a creative intervention. Berger suggests that although "-urgies" have proliferated with the rise of the mass media to the detriment of "-logies," complementarity rather than combat should be sought between them in the face of the problematization of disciplined knowledge posed by the communications revolution with its demands for interdisciplinarity and "involvement."

Ultimately, for Berger (1972: 412) "semiology . . . must be coupled with a 'semiurgy' which . . . participates in the production of signs, their transmission, in short, in the reality produced by signs." The semiologist must become, then, a creative worker and educator; both a sign reader and maker. By contrast, this is precisely what semiology cannot become in Baudrillard's terms, since the imposition of a model in a so-called "universal semiotic" always implies the model's anteriority *and* finality with regard to whatever content it may structure; semiology is operational in the sense that it is a closed system that is brutally functional. Baudrillard's virulent anti-semiological and anti-structural arguments in the end demand the destruction of the semiurgy. Berger's conception of semiology as "-urgy" (work) is closer to McLuhan's understanding of the indispensability of a "producer-orientation," an "artistic strategy" of making and taking, especially in mass-mediated environments.

Constructive and creative variations on the theme of "semiology" were part of the practice of the Collectif d'art sociologique in Paris in the 1970s. Although Berger cannot strictly speaking be counted among its members, his socio-semiotic interests brought him into contact with the group's founders (Fred Forest, Hervé Fischer and Jean-Paul Thenot) in their efforts to engage French sociologists on the broad terrain of the relation between art and society. The Collectif first met in 1972 and published its "Manifesto" in *Le Monde* in October 1974. The Collectif was to "function as a clearing house [*une structure d'accueil*] . . . for all those whose research and artistic practice have as their fundamental theme the sociological fact and the relation between art and society" (Fischer *et al.* 1975: 4). The publishing activities of the Collectif brought together McLuhan and some of his early French readers such as Morin, Berger and Jules Gritti. Gritti, for example, developed a sense of semiurgy similar to that of Berger by using Forest's conceptual art, involving communications technologies such as telephones and their social effects as the occasion to pursue two lines of inquiry regarding the practice of semiology. On the one hand, a semiologist may be a *semiologue* who "reconstitutes laboriously, 'scientifically' . . . the codes which rule over communication"; on the other hand, a *semioclaste* "criticizes and denounces the ideologies which insinuate themselves into codes, adhere to them and invest themselves with a sort of constrictive necessity." Gritti continues: "Thus the approach which wants to be scientific searches and brings to light necessity. Does one establish or end the necessity of codes?" (Gritti in Fischer *et al.* 1975: 48). Gritti considers the work of art as a kind of "dew line" – one of McLuhan's key early terms after which he named his newsletter – on the frontier of previous codes, surpassing old codes by establishing new uncodified rules of interpretation. The work of art arrives in advance of cultural codes – it is literally an early warning system stripped of its technico-military specificity and Cold War paranoia in the North American Air Defense system. This notion of invention on the cutting edge requires a semiurgical intervention into the existing codes shaping communication and hence, the artist *qua* semiurgian is a *semioclaste* who scrambles and rewrites the rules of esthetic and social communication.

Recall that the neologism *sémioclastie* (part sign and part "breaking") entered into circulation through Roland Barthes's use of the term in his reflection on the methodological conjunction and respective maturation of ideological criticism and semiological analysis as he practiced them in his *Mythologies*. Long after its original publication in 1957 (most of the little cultural sketches were written as regular columns from 1954 to 1956 in *Les lettres nouvelles*), what remained for Barthes was that no criticism of the bourgeois norm could eschew detailed analysis, but no semiological analysis could be undertaken which did not come to terms with its *semioclastic* elements. That is, semiology never became for Barthes a simple *semioclasty*, a practice that broke signs.

Barthes awoke from the dream of "scientism," of a science of literature in particular, shortly after what is recognized as his final effort scientifically to ground literary analysis with the structural analysis of narrative (thus, after 1966). His ambivalence toward methodological rigor was already evident in a book of the same year *Critique et vérité* (1966), in which he positioned alongside the developing science of the "immense 'sentences'" of literary works the non-scientific production of meaning called criticism and the practice born of desire for and identification with the work, named reading. Beyond the linguistics of the sentence postulated in *Critique et vérité* lay for Barthes a second linguistics of discourse whose object was the language of narrative. Narrative was the object of the structuralist science of narratology, and literature was the privileged vehicle of narrative. By 1970 with the publication of *S/Z*, a landmark study of Honoré de Balzac's short story *Sarrasine*, Barthes's scientistic period had ended. Structural analysis was displaced by a gradual, textual analysis.

The so-called "second Barthes" wrote reflective and aphoristic works marked by the personal and sensual apprehension of the life of textual signs. By the time Barthes accepted the Chair of Literary Semiology at the Collège de France in 1977, semiology had become for him non-scientific and active, an artistic practice in which one savors and plays with signs as so many fictions. Although Gritti found inspiration in Barthes's reflections, the latter in the end preferred *semiotrophy* to *semioclasty*: "Turned toward the sign, semiology is captivated by and receives the sign, treats it and, if need be, imitates it as an imaginary spectacle" (Barthes 1979: 14). Barthesean semiurgy is an artistic practice which "nourishes" signs; it is essentially playful, and follows the lead of signification rather than digging into its depths.

In Berger's work semiurgy is taken literally, since it calls for involvement on the part of semiologists with the popular culture they often decode. Moreover, the mutation of signs is evidence, Berger concludes, of our own mutation, and of the necessity for dynamic, multidimensional approaches sensitive to the characteristics of emerging media. For Berger (1972: 425) in the end holds out the ideal that "signs will shift in the direction of those who take the initiative, of those who combine power and imagination." This does not mean that McLuhan would have concurred with this modified semiology since he had little understanding of and use for this "science." McLuhan's writings animated rather than sanctioned the critical reflections that Berger and Baudrillard directed at the interpretive edifices of semiology and structuralism. Berger's approach to semiology was enhanced positively by McLuhan's writings; Baudrillard's efforts were devoted to the destruction and transgression of semiology, while grudgingly acknowledging McLuhan's significance and rhetorically derogating his work, at least circa 1972, with such mocking references to McLuhan's "usual Canadian-Texan brutalness" and "McLuhan (for memory's sake)." The relationship between Baudrillard and McLuhan is more complex than this, and it is bound up with the rhetoric of nominations for the position of the "French McLuhan" running through the English literature on Baudrillard.

5

MORE McLUHAN THAN McLUHAN

Two of the major Anglophone (British and American) interpreters of the work of Baudrillard, Mike Gane and Douglas Kellner, have nominated him for the position of the "French McLuhan." Any reader of Baudrillard would recognize the important influence McLuhan has had on his work and not fail to notice the various ways in which this influence has manifested itself over the course of Baudrillard's career to date. The nomination elevates rhetorically McLuhan's influence on Baudrillard above the rest, and it is McLuhan's place that Baudrillard comes to occupy for a new generation of readers, for better and for worse.

The title of "French McLuhan" is not awarded to mere followers, to McLuhanites. It is not Cazeneuve, for example, who is called upon to be the "French McLuhan." Perhaps Cazeneuve was much too literally a French McLuhanite in practice and theory to step into a pair of shoes he had already borrowed on numerous occasions. Further, the title would not be awarded a thinker whose work only criticized McLuhan. The person nominated for the position must not only contribute to media studies in its broadest sense. He or she must have already become a media figure, a recognizable name whose ideas have or have had *cachet*. Moreover, that there is a French McLuhan or a "New McLuhan" who is French – for most, it seems, there is only one at a given time – alerts us to a sociological phenomenon not unknown in other circles. Who are the new Beatles? How often have we heard this question? No one seriously asks: Who is the new Plato? The first question finds its sense in the rock and roll of catalogs, charts, sales figures, new products, seasonal marketing, etc. Still, the nomination of a replacement figure is a way of managing the tides of intellectual influence in so-called "media theory" by filling a vacated position. While there are scholarly reasons for the nomination, these have not been conclusive, for the perceived need of a replacement itself satisfies other interests which critical thinking must interrogate. The nomination solves the immediate problem of filling a vacated seat without requiring the permission of the nominee, whose death is not always the reason for opening the floor. The acceptability of the nominee emerges through an informal consensus among critics and readers who, in a way, second the nomination. Objections are raised against this background.

WRITING SYMBOLIC EXCHANGE

In Gane's (1991a) first book on Baudrillard, *Baudrillard: From Critical to Fatal Theory*, he quotes George Steiner's remarks on the problem McLuhan himself posed to his readers – that is, how to read him, given both his style and the designscape of his publications. Gane thinks it is "instructive" to refigure this problem on behalf of Baudrillard for his readers. He approaches the issue with the claim:

> It would be possible to argue that Baudrillard is the French McLuhan, or simply the McLuhan of today . . . But who reads McLuhan now? Perhaps Baudrillard will force people to reread a number of writers – McLuhan, Nietzsche – who are often thought to be unreadable.
>
> (Gane 1991a: 3)

Gane's nomination is full of hedges. It places his readers in the paradoxical position of wondering whether there will be anyone in the near or distant future who will provoke one to reread Baudrillard. This is very much like asking: who will be the next Baudrillard? Like McLuhan, however, Baudrillard poses for Gane the problem of writing as a symbolic practice. Gane (1991a: 13) adds: "As Baudrillard adopts the full force of McLuhan's notion that the medium is the message, it is to be expected that the medium of the writing style is considered tactically and strategically." Further references to McLuhan appear sporadically in Gane's text. In Gane's (1991b) second book on Baudrillard, *Baudrillard's Bestiary*, there is little emphasis on McLuhan beyond a summary of Baudrillard's (1967) review of McLuhan's *Understanding Media*, in which he rehearsed criticisms of McLuhan in the air in France at the time. What does it mean for Baudrillard to adopt the "full force" of McLuhan's most famous slogan "the medium is the message"? In *La société de consommation*, for instance, Baudrillard (1970: 189) translated this slogan into the differential logic of structural value, arguing that it is not content that is consumed, but rather, the coded semiological relations of successive and equivalent signs divorced from real referents; the slogan has, however, many other meanings in Baudrillard's writings. There is no simple way of accounting for the "full force" of Baudrillard's use of the famous slogan.

Gane's initial nomination, then, acclimatizes readers of Baudrillard to the issue of how his texts establish the critique of the order of simulation from the viewpoint of the symbolic. This critique is said to require specific writing practices beyond the adoption of key terms from the anthropological literature such as "potlatch." Symbolic challenges to the semiological order of simulation are developed textually through a variety of concepts (agonistic relations, anagrammatic dispersion, wit, resocialization of death as a counter-gift), all of which serve to annul systems of value (Marxian, semiological, psychoanalytic). Gane's reference to Baudrillard's style suggests that what is peculiar to his writing of the symbolic is the ambivalence of his texts.[1] It is not merely that one might respond ambivalently to them, but that they are themselves full of ambivalence; in fact, ambivalence is a key concept in the work of the symbolic because it cannot be positivized and positioned as a stable entity in a digital logic of value, unlike ambiguity, for instance. Indeed, Baudrillard's relation to McLuhan is itself full of ambivalence.

There was little attention paid to Baudrillard's style of writing before Gane's suggestions. This does not mean that it was an issue lost on Baudrillard's readers. When such a consideration was raised, it pointed in one direction – toward science fiction. Baudrillard was adopted by the theorists and practitioners of cyberpunk in the same spirit that has recently elevated McLuhan to the status of a patron saint of *Wired* magazine, among other manifestations in glossy print of hypertextual experiments and the possibilities afforded by the development of virtual reality systems. For instance, Istvan Csicsery-Ronay (1988, 1991) has referred to Baudrillard as a philosopher of cyberpunk and a practitioner of cybercriticism, both stylistically and substantively. Baudrillard has at times encouraged these comparisons. In an interview in *Le Monde*, Baudrillard (1984a) suggested that his essay on Beaubourg was a vision from science fiction. Baudrillard's interest in the novels of J. G. Ballard, Arthur C. Clarke and Philip K. Dick is not surprising given the claims advanced in *Simulacres et simulations* (1981b) regarding the (con)fusion of science fiction and theory, and the idea that the real has become science fictional, especially in America with its Hollywood presidents such as Ronald Reagan and its Spielbergesque military programs. Both McLuhan and Baudrillard are looked upon as figureheads in the emergence of virtual reality technologies and infobahns, since the former provided a set of basic figures of electronic globalism pointing toward current developments, and the latter developed a sophisticated language with which to describe the most advanced *simulative* capabilities of new information systems.

The curious simulacral forms populating Dick's (1964) novel *The Simulacra* – the simulacral president and the simulacrum of an "extinct" Martian creature called a papoola which is used to instill by thought projection the desire for commodities, in this case used vehicles, in unsuspecting customers – fit comfortably into the universe Baudrillard describes. In *L'échange symbolique et la mort*, Baudrillard (1976: 305–6) makes explicit use of Clarke's *Les neuf milliards de noms de Dieu* as an instance of anagrammatic resolution – symbolic writing in the poetic mode. The poetic resolution of the world in this novel, and the intense pleasure resulting from an enunciation without remainder, turns on the complete recitation of the nine billion names of God. Here salvation is electronic, since the task is facilitated by a computer, even though in the end Baudrillard claims that the computer spoils the epiphany because it enables one to retrieve the names.

Gane takes up Baudrillard's concept of anagrammatic resolution without remainder in a short chapter in *Baudrillard's Bestiary*. His explication of

Ferdinand de Saussure's anagrams closely follows Jean Starobinski's (1979) presentation of the unpublished manuscripts. In addition, in his *Bestiary* Gane (1991b: 121–25) reads anagrammatically Baudrillard's little-known book of poetry *L'ange de stuc* (1978b) and locates the sounds of the theme words of "Saussure" and "Mauss" in certain stanzas. Gane's work on Saussure's anagrams does not develop his earlier claim in his first book that Baudrillard's writing of the symbolic is McLuhanesque; nor does Gane pursue Baudrillard's criticism of Starobinski's reading of the anagrams along what he perceives to be semio-linguistic lines. McLuhan's phrase "the medium is the message" is, however, closely tied to the concept of the theme word and its circulation.

A poet may draw phonic fragments from a theme word. These fragments are diffracted throughout a poem. For Baudrillard, there is nothing reclaimable about the theme since its identity cannot be resurrected. The intense symbolic circulation of the fragments exterminates the theme; it can be rearticulated but not reconstituted. Baudrillard's distinction between these two concepts is critical to his account of the anagram and his strategy of reading Saussure against himself in order to ensure that this so-called revolutionary poetics will be remainderless. The anagrammatic dispersion of the theme in a poem has, then, nothing left over; there is nothing to accumulate and subsequently subject to a structural linguistic law of value. This dispersion itself guarantees theoretically at least that "the medium is the message," since there is neither a missing or latent reference nor key of some sort remaining to supplement the message. Rearticulation is symbolically acceptable, whereas reconstitution is simulacral.

Baudrillard's reading of Saussure's anagrams, like his use of Sigmund Freud's concept of the *Witz*, emphasizes that the medium cannot be separated from the message; if this were possible, the medium could be subordinated to the demands of depth models of meaning in which disclosure and analysis may be interminable. Media – by which Baudrillard here means the techniques of joking and poetry – are completely resolvable: the technique or medium is their message. Baudrillard's use of McLuhan's phrase is in the service of these expressions of the symbolic, their destruction of meaning and annihilation of the hermeneutic relevance of linguistic and psychoanalytic systems of value. This is not so much an argument against content as it is an attack on what Baudrillard calls "depth models" of interpretation. The symbolic exchange anti-value of the phrase "the medium is the message" supports a revolutionary poetics the possibility of which neither Saussure nor Freud fully recognized in their concepts of the anagram and the *Witz*.

Baudrillard (1978a: 40–41) once again picks up this argument in *A l'ombre des majorités silencieuses*. The question for Baudrillard is whether or not the masses can function in the mode of the symbolic by preferring the fascination of the medium over the domain of meaning. The terms of this "probe" are McLuhanesque, but the stakes are quite different: is it possible to communicate, Baudrillard (1978a: 41) asks, *"outside of the medium of meaning"*? The very idea is untenable, Baudrillard observes. But the neutralization of meaning expressed in the operation of wit is the example which Baudrillard cites in this text, but not only in order to support the obvious observation that McLuhan prophesied the rise of a cool phase of mass culture. Rather, for Baudrillard McLuhan could not have foreseen the symbolic possibilities of his slogan "the medium is the message." The medium is the message that fascinates the masses. They have no interest in the message of the medium because meaning and communication, according to Baudrillard, are neutralized in the mass form's fascination with the medium itself. McLuhan was therefore blind to the most radical effects of his slogans. This places McLuhan beside Freud and Saussure in Baudrillard's eyes.

A second set of issues at stake in my investigation of Baudrillard's writing of the symbolic revolves around design. Baudrillard's efforts at expressing the symbolic in print form did not require the construction of a concrete essay, to use the term used by Theall (1971: 240–41) in his *The Medium Is the Rearview Mirror* to describe the manner in which various typefaces, layouts and visual juxtapositions adhere together in the service of furthering the theoretical positions and descriptions advanced in the text they accompany. Baudrillard's longstanding interest in design, taken together with his participation in the groups centered around the journals *Utopie* and *Traverses*, did lend visual and experimental elements to some of his early essays. The dialectical relationship between a theory and its expression is at the heart of the concrete essay as McLuhan practiced it with the help of his designers. Baudrillard did not collaborate with a designer such as Harley Parker. Design was, however, considered strategically in the SGPP edition of Baudrillard's (1970) *La société de consommation*; the illustrations were dropped from subsequent pocket-size editions, effectively destroying Baudrillard's most McLuhanesque book-object.

The use of print advertisements and photographs illustrates the abundance of chains of object-signs in the society of consumption and fills the text with a busy amalgam of images in a manner similar to the ambience of what Baudrillard called the "drugstore"; by the same token, this concept is not a gloss upon the images. The text engages the phenomena upon which it reflects. The "drugstore" is a model of a polyvalent commercial complex offering consumers the freedom to design their own everyday environments through the accumulation and combination of homogeneous elements. This deluxe banality is semiurgical: the participatory sign-work of consumption (shopping, using customer services, seeking entertainment in the climate-controlled interiors of malls) equates maximal comfort and satisfaction with the maximal exclusion of the real, the social and history (Baudrillard 1970: 34).

The "show and tell" format of *La société de consommation* attracted the attention of Jean-Claude Giradin (1974: 131, n. 6), for whom the book seemed to guarantee itself a place in the universe of objects it described, despite its author's warnings about the "ambience of repression" in a consumer society in which objects take revenge, slowly, upon those who pursue democracy through them and attempt to alleviate subtle forms of alienation by means of consumption:

> A 16 × 20.5 format, a cover with brocaded borders, the title in gilded letters, this volume adorns itself with a reddish brown jacket on which a car exhibits itself . . . (objective fish-eye photography); a skyscraper is reflected on the hood and windshield (a wink at the secondary degree of mirroring) giving a foretaste of remarkable iconography; and, it is lined with alluring captions by the author which punctuate the text. In short, for about $7.50 people will want to have this book not for what it is, they will thumb through it without reading it, but rather to leave it sitting casually between the hi-fi set and the bottle of Chivas as an element of worship in the strategy of the surrounding . . . where a sign-mate will not delay in setting a trap.

A "reader" would have wanted the book for what it was not, for its semiological interdependencies and the combinatory possibilities presented by the "ambience" of a room pulled together by the brand of scotch favored by jet-setters and swingers, and a book by Baudrillard.

In English translation, Baudrillard's books constitute a fetish system of their own: the pretty Verso edition of *America* (1988b) in its time called forth Batman paraphernalia and healing crystals, and beckoned a coffee table on which to display itself and exalt its owner, like an obedient pet; the Agitac edition of Baudrillard's (1988a) *Xerox and Infinity* appeared as a chapbook, a photocopied text waiting to be reproduced in turn; *Seduction* (1990a) is itself fatal in the sense of being irresistible. With its shocking pink cover featuring Man Ray's photograph *Femme aux longs cheveux* framed with vertical green bands which contribute to the overall vibration of this restless jacket, Marilouise Kroker's design is a lesson in seduction, the key terms of which were culled from Baudrillard's text and expressed in formal terms in the book's design, effectively fetishizing Baudrillard for Francophiles. Not even Baudrillard recognized himself in this book-object. In English translation, then, Baudrillard has been McLuhanized to the degree that several of his essays and books were rendered in the manner of the concrete essay.

The estheticized recommodification of Baudrillard for Anglophone audiences has all but ignored consideration of those texts in which Baudrillard's writings have been accompanied by images. It is not only that the illustrated edition *La société de consommation* has not been translated, but the original is long out of print. Good examples of journal articles were available for more than ten years in *Traverses*, the Revue trimestrielle du Centre de création industrielle published by the Centre Georges Pompidou, in whose pages essays by Baudrillard were illustrated along thematic lines. Earlier and more interesting examples may be found in his contributions to the journal *Utopie, Revue de sociologie de l'urbain*. The large format of the first two issues (1967 and 1969) accommodated typographic heterogeneity and simple uses of collage (clustering and stacking of images of objects and, on occasion, pop art-inspired graphics expressing the violent explosion of the alienated and hitherto dominated masses). *Utopie*'s design did not follow straightforwardly from McLuhan's praise of collage, whether it was in terms of the Global Village understood as an "animated collage," or as the participatory spirit created by a Happening read as a kind of theater of the electronic age (McLuhan and Watson 1970: 198–99).

Baudrillard did not uncritically adopt McLuhan's praise for collage and "participation." During the 1960s, claims upon collage (and Happenings) were made from several political camps. For example, the German playwright Peter Weiss, four of whose plays Baudrillard translated into French in the 1960s, used collage as a means of breaking through the artificial universe of the media. Documentary theater "cuts and pastes" existing documentary material in order to re-edit mainstream mediatic representations of current events, revealing the latent conflicts, falsifications and political-corporate interests shaping the presentation of information to the public. Documentary theater resists the implosive electronic-oral-aural consciousness heralded by McLuhan by engaging in subdivision and segmentation, which were for him outmoded ways of thinking. Weiss's resistance stands alongside the Situationists' attacks on Happenings (the negation of the Happening understood as a negation of naturalistic theater) as spectacles diametrically opposed to the creation of a situation by means of the subversive appropriation and recontextualization of existing materials. Still, even such *détournements* could be reproduced as news or as performance art, losing their critical and transformative edges as diversionary tactics. This is a view expressed in similiar terms by the Canadian composer R. Murray Schafer. Recently, Schafer has reflected on a remark he made in 1972 with respect to the "messy excretions" of what was called total theater:

> There is no reason to retract this assertion, despite the recent growth of picture books in which various experiments in . . . total theatre are presented as if they were substantive or repetitive contributions to art. They are documents only, smoothed down photographically and multiplied in quantity to give the contemporary public – who prefer illusions – the impression that something has happened. But the essence of a "happening" . . . is its nonrepeatability.
>
> (Schafer 1991: 29, n.3)

The spectacularization and repetition of situations was not lost on the Situationists: their work was also subjected to the manufacture of alienation and the self-affirming and self-justifying economy of the spectacle.

WHAT IS PARTICIPATION?

Kellner (1989: 73) writes that "Baudrillard can be seen as a 'new McLuhan' who has repackaged McLuhan into new postmodern cultural capital." Kellner's nomination of Baudrillard for the post of the "new McLuhan" is a meta-rhetorical arrangement in the following sense. The results of this arrangement (the rhetorical use of a rhetorical nomination) are treated by Kellner as a trio of "subordinations" shared by Baudrillard and McLuhan: content and use are subordinate to form; dialectical analysis is subordinate to essentialism and technological determinism; context-specific cultural analyses and alternative political formations are subordinate to a romantic and nostalgic sense of theory. These "subordinations" occlude, Kellner maintains, a critical discussion of the sort of issues he deems apposite but which are absent from McLuhan's work and from Baudrillard's as well (i.e., an analysis of the political economy of media production; an entry into a dialectical reading of form with content and media with society).

What makes Kellner's nomination of Baudrillard meta-rhetorical is that the "subordinations" are themselves subordinate to the arguments advanced in the early 1970s by Fekete (1973) against McLuhan, which Kellner rehearses, but this time directing them against Baudrillard. The nomination, then, makes possible this kind of substitution of targets. Simply put, Baudrillard is branded as a new "McLuhanatic" (a lunatic and counter-revolutionary) collaborating with "the system," making a fetish of technology, especially television, and furthering the passivity, alienation and domination of consumers by the conservative media-business elites of advanced capitalism. Fekete's use of the derogatory term "McLuhanacy" linked eccentricity with culpability – McLuhan was not so "unsound" as to be considered incapable before the new Left – and furthered a rhetorical practice of discrediting McLuhan already in circulation by the mid-1960s (Behar and Libermann 1968). The term referred both to the enthusiasm of McLuhan's followers, thereby diminishing these people's mental capacities by branding them as irrational members of a cult, and to McLuhan's own penchant for wit, paradox and glib talk. The "Cult of McLuhanacy" was a precursor of the "Baudrillard Scene" on the level of a pop-philosophical phenomenon; the latter has certainly not lacked intimations of mind control and feeble-mindedness. Some of Baudrillard's (1983) French critics have called his work "unreadable" and "schizophrenic."

One of the effects of Kellner's nomination is to render moot comparative and contrastive textual insights into the Baudrillard–McLuhan ligature. Why? According to Kellner, nothing has changed from McLuhan to Baudrillard. For instance, Kellner (1989:70) notes that in his "later writings" Baudrillard adopts literary practices similar to those of McLuhan (probes and mosaic constellations of images and concepts) which prevent the articulation of a "well-defined theoretical position." Unlike Gane, Kellner does not connect these "McLuhanite" strategies with Baudrillard's project of establishing the symbolic as a revolutionary concept with which to challenge the one-dimensional society of simulations; neither does the mention of such strategies suggest the variety of uses Baudrillard finds for McLuhan's concepts. In order to secure the nomination on behalf of Baudrillard, Kellner downplays the theoretical significance of the anti-semiological and anti-simulational concept of the symbolic in its so-called "early" and "later" manifestations. There is no equivalent concept in McLuhan's work. McLuhan's notions find a place in Baudrillard's work in relation to his own most important but least critically recognized concept of the symbolic and its manifestations. Kellner himself demonstrates the consequences of defining a theoretical "position": the production of a fog of sameness in which critical investigation loses itself.

It would be pointless to deny, however, that there is a superficial resemblance in the relation expressed by McLuhan's idea of participation and Baudrillard's concept of symbolic exchange. The concept of participation is subject to general critical remarks in Baudrillard's *Le miroir de la production* (1973). As McLuhan (1964: 22–24) explained in *Understanding Media*, media are extensions of psychic and sensory capacities. A hot medium (photography and radio) extends a single sense in "high definition," that is, one filled with data. A cool or "low definition" medium (telephone and television) provides a meager amount of information and extends several senses at once. Hot media are low, while cool media are high in participation, which is defined in terms of what a receiver has to bring to the medium to complete its message: more involvement means the medium is "inclusive"; a less involving medium is "exclusive."

The concept of symbolic exchange takes many forms in Baudrillard's writings. It is in general incommensurable with any system of value. It is in addition anti-productivist and involves the sumptuary destruction of signs; in this respect it is potlatch-like, and thought to be governed by obligation and agonistic reciprocity of gift exchange, returning what is given or destroyed in kind or with interest. The fatal malady of capitalism is, Baudrillard argues, its inability to reproduce itself symbolically. Yet capital, understood as a code, can and does simulate symbolic processes by admitting as differential value every form of liberation, no matter how strange such social movements and initially non-marked forces make it seem to itself. Like McLuhan, Baudrillard valorizes, by means of an explicit archaism, so-called primitive and tribal cultures. While McLuhan gleefully announces the retribalization of the post-Gutenbergian world, Baudrillard uses "primitive" practices to attack the highest order of simulation. Both eschew ethnographic detail for the sake of their dominant conceptual figures. In some instances, their views momentarily converge. For McLuhan practical jokes and aphorisms are physically and mentally involving. Baudrillard, too, treats jokes and aphorisms as cool phenomena.

These convergences quickly break down since for Baudrillard (1973: 125) participation reproduces the system of the capitalist code. For participation "has a connotation that is much too contractual and rationalist to express what is symbolic" (1973: 123). Baudrillard attempts to explain that the code of capital integrates a symbolic variable under the rubric of participation, as sign-value. In spite of this, Baudrillard still holds out the symbolic's radical, irreducible alterity in the forms of the incessant circulation of speech, which takes responsibility for itself and the personal relations it cements; the festive destruction of riches elevating the element of ritual exhaustion contained in Baudrillard's injunction that "signs must burn" over consumption, used by Baudrillard in sociological terms in such phrases as "la société de consommation" (consumer society) and as a metaphysical principle as in "la consommation de la consommation" (the consumption of consumption); and the release of anti-productive potential against the structural inability of systems defined by their internal logic to realize human potential other than in terms of productive forces. It makes little difference for Baudrillard that McLuhan is thought of as a dupe of capital, since the alternative offered by Marxism (including Marxist critiques of McLuhan) is itself mired in the simulation of the mandate of production and the projection of its categories onto "primitive" societies. Baudrillard, albeit unwillingly, commits a similar projection in the name of the symbolic akin to McLuhan's (1964: 40) own myth of the anxiety-free state of "backward and nonindustrial countries" whose very backwardness and coolness prepare them for the electric revolution. While McLuhan recognized that the arrival of electric technologies created a series of minor irritations (anxiety and boredom), there is nothing quite as volatile as the "break and entry" of the Baudrillardian symbolic into the semiurgy, at least in theory.

Inspired by McLuhan's focus on the medium, the experimental artist Fred Forest received permission from *Le Monde* in 1972 to provide a 150 sq cm blank space in one issue of the newspaper in which readers could "speak in response" to the largely unidirectional messages (Fischer 1976: 213–14). Some 800 responses were returned to the artist. Forest repeated this exercise in several other media, including radio and television. By opening a space for the responses of readers, Forest did not break what Baudrillard calls the "fundamental rule of non-response of all media." Forest's experiment is an example of what Baudrillard (1972: 228) calls "fragile manipulatory practices" that do not challenge the medium but, rather, stage responses in terms the medium can accommodate. In this case, the newspaper served as a medium in the sense of an intermediary channel for the delivery of letters to the artist, and maintained the abstract separateness of its readers and their mode of participation.

Baudrillard's general critical remarks on participation do not, however, address McLuhan's specific claims about the media user's involvement with cool and hot media. Nonetheless, Baudrillard's general remarks on participation cast a shadow of doubt over McLuhan's version of the seminal concept. In an article coauthored with de Kerckhove on television and radio for the *Encyclopedia universalis* (France), McLuhan (1968: 898–99) maintains that television totally engages the viewer. One is involved in a "process of configuration that is always in progress" with regard to the relatively small number of the luminous points on the screen out of which the image is, according to this "perceptualist" position, constructed. Theorizing against the etymological grain of tele-vision as the domain of the eye, the active participation of the viewer is primarily tactile, a concept defined constitutively in terms of the interplay of all the senses. The television viewer takes an interior trip that appears by external criteria to be one that is passive. Even so, the idea that one is glued to the screen brings home McLuhan's fascination with the tactility of the television experience. This interior voyage of the central nervous system into the magnetic field gives television its communal flavor and puts it on a continuum with the psychedelic drug trip. There are no bad trips in the cool world of McLuhan-vision. The case of television is the most extreme and the most important example of participatory experience in McLuhan's writings.

Baudrillard understands participation ideologically in the context of his critique of models of communication that merely simulate communication, usually by means of consumption. His approach does not illumine the specific problems of McLuhan's definition, but succeeds in drawing attention to the ideological nature of participation in general, which in its turn may be used to reconsider certain ambiguities and problems in McLuhan's account. Francis Balle (1972) took precisely this tack in his book *Pour comprendre les médias: MacLuhan*. Participation became a buzzword of sorts and circulated widely in the late 1960s and early 1970s according to various theories of "unfinished" or "open" works, especially the *nouveau cinéma* and *roman* of Alain Resnais and Alain Robbe-Grillet, respectively. The destruction of linear narrative placed new demands on audiences. But the polysemic fluctuations of the term have emptied it, Balle claims, of all signification, since it is not clear whether it concerns the messages conveyed, their stylistic differences and the conditions of reception, or the use made of a given medium. Balle continues: "We never know on which of these three levels MacLuhan situates his observations; moreover, the examples which serve as illustrations show, rather, that he passes from one to the other without paying attention to them" (Balle 1972: 56). Further, Balle thinks the distinction between cool and hot media expresses McLuhan's hostility toward print culture and has little to do with verifiable insights: "the distinction has been put to work only to justify the disrepute into which the techniques and the arts contemporary to the age of print at one and the same time have fallen" (Balle 1972: 58). The cool/hot typology is ideological, Balle asserts, because it substitutes values for facts and desire and fear for empirical observations of the media. McLuhan's sociology of the media is in the service of his prophetism or, in other words, *media* serve the interests and preferences of the *médium* himself.

Earlier I showed how McLuhan's most famous slogan supported Baudrillard's understanding of anagrammatic dispersion and the *Witz* in *L'échange symbolique*. *L'échange symbolique* is often considered the last book of Baudrillard's "early writings," after which, it would appear, he adopted more fully McLuhan's ideas, if we are to believe his critics. But this conventional reading tells us little about the details of Baudrillard's appropriations of McLuhan's work. What it does not tell us is that *L'échange symbolique* was not translated into English in its entirety until 1993, precisely 17 years after it first appeared. There are still no studies of this important, indeed pivotal, text available for English readers. One can only imagine what the "Baudrillard Scene" would have looked like if this important book had appeared before the terms postmodernist and Baudrillard became synonymous.[2]

Turning again to *L'échange symbolique*, Baudrillard grafts McLuhan's distinction between hot and cool media onto the logic of the sign's reference. In a hot and referential semiological regime, the medium is not the message. When the medium becomes the message, one enters the cool era of operational simulation, Baudrillard writes (1976: 41), an era characterized semiologically by the referentless Saussurean signs of the structural revolution of value. Monetary signs are cool for Baudrillard: affectless, commutable, tied to the rules of the structural system, and unconnected with parasystemic real referents. Money has not, however, become only a medium whose circulation and disconnectedness is its message: "It is no longer a medium, a means for the circulation of goods, it is the *circulation itself*, that is to say, the realized form of the system in its abstract rotation" (Baudrillard 1976: 41). Money is, then, a kind of pure movement, a hyper-medium. Julian Pefanis (1991: 63; 141, n.13) draws attention to Baudrillard's parodic and subversive use of McLuhan's concepts in this passage. But Pefanis's additional passing remark that this reference rescues McLuhan from some "oblivion" lacks a critical and historical context. Baudrillard's use of "coolness" in this passage adheres to an often neglected aspect of the concept which McLuhan (1969c) specified in terms of "rending" and "wracking." Cool money is circulation itself, liberated from both use value and exchange value, and thus relieved of exchangist messages. It is its own message. This disconnected kind of money has, then, the power to "rend and wrack" any national economy, Baudrillard adds (1976: 41), because it is no longer tied to a market, to a local equilibrium, to a mode of production, to a common measure, etc. Cool money relates only to itself, "participates" in its own inflationary spiral and periodic crashes, and it surpasses, as McLuhan himself noted and Baudrillard emphasizes, in its abstractness and the speed at which it moves, hot hardware and even credit, with anarchic consequences.

There is yet another way to appreciate Baudrillard's interrogation of participation as a form of simulation. Consider, for a moment, the third hypothesis regarding the social that Baudrillard advanced in *A l'ombre* (1978a: 86ff.): "The social has well and truly existed, but it no longer exists." Social contracts and "relations" in general between state and civil society, public and private domains, groups and individuals, give way to mere contacts. The social is reduced to a telephatic functionality: points of contact, information processing and exchange, a generalized connectivity, encoding and decoding ruled over by a digital code (0/1). The perspectival space of the social gives way to the space of simulation in which the real is confused with simulacral models. In this confusion there is a loss of critical distance. A few years earlier in *L'échange symbolique* (1976: 96ff.), Baudrillard explained the loss of critical distance in terms borrowed directly from McLuhan. In the referendum mode of life, digitality has invaded everything. The most concrete form of digitality is the test. Under non-stop testing, there is no distance for critical reflection; there is no time for reaction and reformulation (later in this chapter I will show how Virilio teases out the military implications of the loss of reaction time). This is a portrait of participation in the third order of simulation. A selectively encoded message captures "reality" in terms of a question/answer to which one is required to respond or decode by selecting one of the two terms presented. The testing mode is a form of constant contact or tactile communication. McLuhan, Baudrillard (1976: 100) remarks, correctly diagnosed the tactility of the electronic mass media. Tactility results from the loss of distance between question and answer in a world saturated with testing, probing, polling and sampling. Herein, Baudrillard thinks, the "message becomes a 'massage,' a tentacular solicitation."

Baudrillard's attention to McLuhan is for the most part limited to textual skirmishes with certain slogans and concepts. He often stretches the limits of concepts such as cool and hot. This tactic involves, for instance, the infusion of a recurring issue in his writing, such as the flotation of money and of signs without referential anchors with McLuhan's concepts. This infusion neither elucidates the concepts nor does it always add substantively to the issue at hand. Rather, they are introduced with a calculated abandon, quickly saturating an issue so as to heighten the sense that it is perfecting itself and in so doing spiralling out of control; and this applies to Baudrillard as well: more McLuhan than McLuhan.

Baudrillard's working hypothesis with respect to the slogan "the medium is the message" is, on the one hand, that McLuhan's "prophecy" has been realized. This acknowledgment does not mean that Baudrillard supports this state of affairs. On the contrary, this hypothesis is a first step toward pushing the terms of the slogan to the very limits of sense in order to describe the development of media in a society of simulations. On the other hand, the hypothesis that McLuhan was right and remains more correct than he perhaps should have been is an exaggeration which Baudrillard hopes will, in a second step, destabilize the very development the slogan captures. Baudrillard has attempted to theorize this "final straw" (the straw that broke "the system's" back) by various means throughout his career. He continued to use the revolutionary rhetoric of beating "the system" into the mid-1970s, even though by this time "the system" in question was defined structurally and included diverse phenomena such as models of communication and the power of biocrats to control the distinction between life and death from the Thanatos centers of the hospital and the laboratory. Paradoxically, McLuhan's slogan defines the field against which symbolic violence must be applied, *and* simultaneously may be used to read Freud and Saussure against themselves, thereby articulating certain modes of symbolic exchange. This is the central tension in Baudrillard's use of McLuhan's ideas: the slogan "the medium is the message" is radical and not very radical. This is, I think, the "fullest force" of the phrase in Baudrillard's writings.

A further, clearly parodic way of acknowledging McLuhan appears in Baudrillard's (1992: 17) notion of "the generalization of McLuhan's theory of the 'extensions of man'." The emphasis on electronic extensions of the brain has reached, Baudrillard thinks, a critical point of reversal in which the brain becomes an "extension" or internal prosthetic device of the body. The prosthetic brain is internal to the body but no longer centered by it. It seems to be pursuing an orbit independent of its individual body! It is at this point that Baudrillard denies he is writing science fiction. It is purely parodic to suggest that McLuhan's well-known optimism about technological extensions of bodies has resulted in the concentric orbit of these extensions around the bodies from which they were launched. Baudrillard's reason for this travesty is clear enough: he claims that it is the work of theory to play a game of one-upmanship, of going to extremes with the goal of destabilizing existing systems and theories. Baudrillard's guiding principle is, as McLuhan believed, breakdown as breakthrough, though he does not subscribe to the hypothesis that a hitherto unacknowledged depth may be disclosed through an inter-ruption drawing attention to the medium. Rather, for Baudrillard the code is challenged by a symbolic violence which consists in returning to it the principle of its own power (the power to give unilaterally without return), thereby driving it to a point of breakdown because it can neither respond nor retort except by its own collapse (Baudrillard 1976: 64–65). The counter-gift returned to the code is an initiatic form of death (see Genosko 1998). In addition, the symbolic enters the semiurgical universe with the violence of a break and entry, an *effraction*. In Baudrillard's theorizing breakdown takes the form of a break-in.

There is also an important unmarked allusion to McLuhan in Baudrillard's *Amérique*. The three orders of simulation which Baudrillard explained in *L'échange symbolique* reappear a decade later in *Amérique* (1986) with one finely tuned difference. Baudrillard's well-known model of the orders of simulacra has three parts (until a fourth order was added in *La transparence du mal* (1990b)). Briefly, then, the first order is that of the counterfeit. It marked the emergence in the Renaissance of exogamous and democratic relations between signs emancipated from their referential obligations. The second order of the industrial simulacrum arose with the Industrial Revolution. The simulation of original referents is replaced by the law of general equivalence involving the production of a pure series of identical objects subject to market forces. The third order of structural simulation is a post-industrial phenomenon. Mechanical reproduction is transcended in the conception of signs and objects in terms of their reproducibility. This order is dominated by what Baudrillard calls the "code": the rules governing the combinatorial possibilities of the terms of a closed system and the appointment and holding of their relations in an abstract separateness. Baudrillard suggests that in America there is no second order of simulation; hence, he suggests, on the basis of his wide-ranging descriptions of the three stages (here given in psycho-philosophical language, whereas elsewhere he prefers economic, sometimes semiotic, technological codings, and even the language of physics), the absence of an industrial simulacrum based upon the dominant form of production regulated by the market. Baudrillard writes (1986: 208):

> What is new in America is the clash of the first level (primitive and wild) and the third stage (the absolute simulacrum). There is no second level. This is a situation difficult for us [Europeans] to understand since we have always privileged the second level, the reflexive, split personality, the unhappy consciousness.

In Baudrillard's America, the first and third orders of simulation collide to produce a real fiction, given the transitive relations of the orders in what was once an intransitive model. The mystery of American reality is that it is hyperreal: it reverses European values and cultural categories, elevating the simulacrum over the ideal and the materialization of utopia over its possibility. The idea that a country such as the United States did not experience a phase of history in its development – contrary to appearances – was used by McLuhan in the mid-1960s to describe the situation of *les Québécois* in the Province of Québec in Canada. Something, in other words, is missing from Baudrillard's America and McLuhan's Québec.

In 1965, McLuhan sought to explain French Canadian nationalism in terms of the age of electricity. Cultural decentralization was, McLuhan held, a normal consequence of the general decentralization of the electric age of instantaneity. In Québec this took the form of a cultural-political-linguistic nationalism and separatist politics. In McLuhan's initial estimation, the rebirth of Québécois culture was permitted by the present age (Kattan 1965). By 1967, however, McLuhan theorized that *les Québécois* were people of the seventeenth century, and therefore tribal and feudal. Unlike their English counterparts, French Canadians did not experience the nineteenth century (nor, for that matter, McLuhan thought, did they have an eighteenth century). McLuhan (1987: 351) once wrote in all seriousness to the then Prime Minister of Canada, Pierre Trudeau, that "French Canadians never had a nineteenth century." English and French Canadians had difficulty understanding one another because the nineteenth-century message of the Anglophone was received by a seventeenth-century Quebecker; that is, French Canadians find it hard to understand the mechanical, specialist and rigid orientation of Anglo-Canadians. The greatest threat to Québécois cultural and political self-determination and freedom was, McLuhan believed, the industrialization and urbanization of French Canadian society (n.a. 1967b). These Francophone "hippies" were perfectly adapted to the twentieth century, as the mosaic called Expo '67 in Montréal revealed, at least for McLuhan; it is useful to recall that McLuhan was launched into French orbit at the Québec Pavilion during Expo '67. Despite the lack of a common experience, McLuhan opined, Expo '67 provided the opportunity for dialogue between English and French Canadians. These remarks about "seventeenth-century hippies" contributed to McLuhan's downfall in Québec, despite the best efforts of his translator and promoter Jean Paré, among others, to provide him with opportunities to retract his statements. I will take up McLuhan's rise and fall in Québec in greater detail in Chapter 6.

It needs to be remembered that Baudrillard was, circa 1967, critical of McLuhan's work, focussing on the illogicality of the hot–cool distinction and the perilous and paradoxical slogan "the medium is the message." McLuhan's optimism is based on "the total misunderstanding of the history and, to be precise, the social history of media" (Baudrillard 1967: 229). McLuhan's misunderstanding results from his use of what Baudrillard calls a "binary typology" of hot and cool media, around which he organized the triphasic model of history: a cool pre-literate tribalism – a hot Gutenbergian galaxy – a cool electric, post-literate, neo-tribal age. While McLuhan's thesis is worked through in a more or less logical way, its terms are, Baudrillard claims in concert with many others of his fellow French readers of McLuhan, "illogical and ambiguous." First, McLuhan does not define the sort of "participation" at issue in his definition of cool culture. Baudrillard wonders whether this participation is passive, a matter of an emotional investment, perhaps even of the order of "addiction" to television, or active, involving an intellectual or contemplative attitude. One doesn't look the same way, Baudrillard remarks, at kinetic art as one does at a painting by Vermeer. The term "cool" doesn't permit one to make fine distinctions around the sort of "curiosity" aroused by such diverse works. Despite these objections, Baudrillard expresses his interest in the hitherto poorly understood consequences of the introduction of hot media into cool cultures (radio into non-Westernized communities) and cool media into hot cultures (television into book culture).

As far as slogans go, Baudrillard (1967: 229) claims, "the medium is the message" is as false and reductionistic as any other. But it must not be ignored. For McLuhan is claiming that, in Baudrillard's terms, the book-object has transformed civilization in virtue of "the fundamental constraint of systematization that it exercises through its technical essence" rather than through its ideological content. Media are "technical objects" that reshape human relations. "The message of television," Baudrillard maintains:

> is not found in the images it broadcasts but in the new modes of relation and perception that it imposes, and which change the traditional structures of the family. Further still, in the case of tv: what is received, consumed, assimilated – thus the real message – is much less this or that spectacle than the virtuality of the succession of all possible spectacles. This is the tv-object, the tv-medium: it has precisely the effect (if not the function) of neutralizing the lived, unique and occurrent character of what it transmits, making of its programs a discontinuous "message" consisting of signs juxtaposed in the abstract dimension of the broadcast.
>
> (Baudrillard 1967: 229–30)

What Baudrillard is describing is a seriality-effect of sameness that puts an end to the idea that the televisual message has a referent, instead inserting it in a chain in which images of war, for example, have a "transitive" or direct relation with – to employ Baudrillard's vocabulary – other kinds of images such as those of advertising rather than to real events. What Baudrillard is claiming here is that television is a harbinger of the structural revolution of value. In an attempt to take McLuhan's concepts in a slightly different, but related, direction, Baudrillard adds that messages refer to other messages and media refer to other media. The other media to which the tv-object refers are the images it transmits, and these images may also refer to other objects. This relation is context dependent. Baudrillard contrasts the effects of television in an unspecified "Africa" as opposed to the West: in the former, the flow of images transmits Western objects; in the latter, the tv-object transmits images. This reciprocity of media amounts to, for Baudrillard (1967: 230), the "totalitarian message of a consumer society."

Over the course of his career Baudrillard has read the formula "the medium is the message" into the logic of sign value, breaking the spell of McLuhan's optimism. Yet optimism returned as Baudrillard came to consider, in the mid-1970s, the slogan in terms complementary to the vehicles of symbolic exchange. This seemingly contradictory usage was followed by his adaptation of McLuhan's notion of a blank spot in historical experience to American society. Scattered throughout Baudrillard's writings one finds instances of parodic extensions of McLuhan's concepts, and places at which their language overlaps. One of the most significant sites is the concept of implosion, to which I now turn.

THE MASTERS OF IMPLOSION

"Implosion" – by which McLuhan meant the "pulling out of the spaces [and time] between components" – is brought about by revolutions in telecommunications, primarily by the speed of new media, and reconfigures "all operations, all information, all associations" (McLuhan 1969a: 12). Echoing the critical literature, Barry Smart (1992: 126–28) remarks that in Baudrillard's hands, McLuhan's "dictum" that the medium is the message works itself out in an emphasis on form, the meaning of which is "far from exhausted." Baudrillard's concern with form (in particular, in his analyses of the object and mass society) culminate for Smart in the implosion of the media and the masses, yielding the Baudrillardian version of the dictum the "mass(age) is the message" rather than McLuhan's version "the medium is the massage." Baudrillard uses his version to show, by contrast, that the mass is a form of implosion refusing socialization. Implosion indicates the catastrophe of the collapse of new media toward the mass form: the mass form does not radiate, instead, it absorbs (expansion is reversed by implosion). For Baudrillard, implosion does not produce the intimacy of the Global Village. The new patterns of inclusive structuration postulated by McLuhan yield their inverse: inertia, silence, indifference. Saturated by communication, human relations are reduced to points of "contact" or "telephasis." Baudrillard here turns McLuhan's sense of implosion inside out, but not toward explosion, by burying it in the indifference of the mass form. This is also, on another level of analysis, precisely how McLuhan (1969c: 8) worked, since he claimed that a kind of proto-Baudrillardian "fatal reversibility" reigns over events: "one of the observations of the I Ching, the *Book of Changes*, some 3,000 years old, is 'when a thing reaches its limit, it turns around' – it reverses its characteristics." Reversibility, or a flip, is a key to Baudrillard's critical practice of reading thinkers against themselves. On a generous reading of the relationship between Baudrillard and McLuhan, one might conclude that the apparent contradictions of Baudrillard's use of McLuhan's concepts are really only examples of a series of flips or inversions as a given concept exhausts itself and reverses its characteristics.

More specifically, Baudrillard's (1978a: 69ff.) hypotheses concerning the social rely on the figure of reversibility, as well as those of reabsorption and recycling. He argues that the development and success of the institutions advancing "socialization" simultaneously mark the destruction and regression of the social. The key figure in this argument is reversibility: all definitions of the social are reversible. As more and more of the social is produced outwardly, it is inwardly neutralized. Outward simulations of the social – especially those emananting from the media – are burying it. While the social is destroyed by the media and information that produce it, it is reabsorbed by what it has produced, namely, the masses. For these reasons Baudrillard claims that the social is an empty term, an alibi of sociologists and socialists alike. The "reverse pattern" was used by McLuhan (1964: 45ff.) to describe the speed-induced flip from explosion to implosion and centralization to decentralization, from the mechanic to the organic. An "overheated medium," to use McLuhan's language, reaches a "saturation point" or "break boundary" beyond which it assumes a new dynamic and direction, usually as a result of overextension through cross-fertilization or interplay. McLuhan's examples are typically wide-ranging, but subsumable under the general principle that "during the stages of their development all things appear under forms opposite to those that they finally present" (McLuhan 1964: 46).

The indifference of the mass form as a kind of resistance has little to do with the paradise of involvement in the social process. Baudrillard considers his own position to be neither pessimistic nor optimistic. It is beyond both of these, involving irony, ruse and antagonism born of the renunciation of political intelligence and rational choice, the loss of interest in self-constitution, self-understanding, productive citizenship and social responsibility. Baudrillard's sense of the mass form is an antidote to sociology: if sociology survives on the positive hypothesis of the social and its expansion, it cannot survive the hypothesis of the implosion and the death of the social. No one can speak, especially sociologists, in the name of the masses.

In *Understanding Media*, McLuhan (1964: 47) wrote:

> The stepping-up of speed from the mechanical to the instant electric form reverses explosion into implosion. In our present electric age the imploding or contracting energies of our world now clash with the old expansionist and traditional patterns of organization.

The terms employed by McLuhan and Baudrillard are identical: McLuhan writes of the shift from explosion to implosion; Baudrillard uses this shift to tell a story about the impossibility of sociology and the end of the social. The reference employed by McLuhan to a traditional organization is retained by Baudrillard as well, although for him it has nothing to do with his romantic conception of symbolic societies that require neither "social relations" nor the simulation of the social. McLuhan's electric form is translated by Baudrillard into a mass form. The electrical usage remains the same, but with Baudrillard the ground has a neutralizing rather than a "tribalizing" effect.

It is not only McLuhan and Baudrillard who have developed the concept of implosion. Implosion is also employed by Virilio, who emphasizes the speed of the collapse of space and time and the vehicles by means of which this is accomplished. In his essay "The Last Vehicle," Virilio (1989b) gathers together a series of diverse examples to illustrate the victory of sedentariness over movement and change: a simulated wave pool, exercise machines, flight simulators, miniature reconstructions − all of which reveal the "advent of inertia" replacing change of place. The last vehicle is a static vehicle, the final mutation of the dynamic vehicle. In this mutation the static and dynamic vehicle become confused: the automotive and the audiovisual implode in the paradoxical priority of the arrival over the departure brought about by the information revolution, telecommunications and the nearly instantaneous presence of places and moments. Automotivity is threatened by the static vehicularity of a completely imploded world in constant communication. The intensive time of vehicular implosion threatens the extensive time of physical transportation. Intensive time is "momentariness without history," an earthly contraction, a contraction of the starting and finishing lines parallel to the ascendancy of the arrival over the departure, in which the scene disappears with the emergence of the screen.

With geographical contraction, chronopolitics supplants geopolitics. Speed supplants place. Places are exterminated, localization is disqualified; again, contraction results in the interfacing of surfaces, "the juxtaposition of every locality" (Virilio 1986: 136). What is destroyed is a field of action, of "buffers" and distance: a radical reduction of reaction time occurs with increases in the speed with which destruction may be delivered or communicated. The "last war" is that of time over space, the triumph of technical improvements in the performances of weapons systems over tactical maneuverability in the perilous drift toward automated decision-making. The "last war" of time is a constant state of emergency in which the present collapses in the "instantaneousness of decision." The reduction of time for political decision-making has been steadily eroded over the course of the last three decades and this entails for Virilio a decrease of freedom, a servitude produced by speed and given over to automation: the war machine itself takes over decision-making as deterrence is automated. The "last decision-maker" will be only a memory of humans held in the memory banks of machines.

All of these descriptions are consonant with McLuhan's hypotheses on speed. All technological extensions of the body increase power and speed, McLuhan maintains, and this is disruptive: "the alteration of social groupings, and the formation of new communities, occurs with the increased speed of information movement" (1964: 91). Power structures are altered by electric and electronic speeds that erase margins and create centers everywhere in a generalized implosive communication, an "instant implosion and an interfusion of space and function" (McLuhan 1964: 93). There is a certain Foucauldian flavor to these observations, to the extent that power appears to be decentered, that is, centers are everywhere and power thus comes from everywhere; McLuhan's emphasis on electricity also hints at an energetics of "force relations." McLuhan was also hypothesizing what he called a "reverse pattern": the population explosion flips into an implosion of population, raising questions about how to live in "utmost proximity" with the rest of the world. And the other side of technologically mediated global awareness is, as every Foucauldian knows, surveillance.

Heterogeneous speeds or discrepancies in speeds of movement existing alongside one another in a given place such as a city, for instance, are conflictual, McLuhan believes, whereas homogeneous speeds entail balance and uniformity. What happens when the military runs ahead of everyone else? "War," McLuhan observed (1964: 101), "is never anything less than accelerated technological change." Implosion and contraction replace explosion and expansion, but the race toward total acceleration is simultaneously a technical drive toward automated decision-making that amputates McLuhan's anchor of the human sensorium and its extensions. The differences between Virilio and McLuhan are profound and best appreciated by considering their respective representations of the drive toward automation.

The global dimension of implosion created for McLuhan a "total field of inclusive awareness." In this total field in which space–time barriers are vaulted, nostalgia develops for older patterns of human interchange. With increased speeds, specialization disappears, as do the old dichotomies of work and leisure, teachers and students. For McLuhan, automation is information instantaneously retrievable by all. Disciplinary boundaries in principle fall; fragmentation is replaced by organic unity; and specific awareness gives way to Gestalt awareness. Automation doesn't extend, in this scenario, mechanization but, rather, it invades it with the "instantaneous character of electricity" (McLuhan 1964: 302). Thinking is equal to doing; linearity is replaced by synchronicity. Automation is the product of "electric instant speeds" and McLuhan conceives of it as the vehicle of implosion whose soft crash, the kiss of fenders, if you will, is an "instant inclusive embrace." Automation is contentless, non-specialist and separate from its translation or application. Electric implosion replaces mechanical explosion. Speed entails the organic interplay of electricity conceived informationally and it mystically illuminates whomever it brings into contact.

McLuhan and Virilio read contraction to dissimilar ends. While Virilio emphasizes the "fearful friction" of implosion, McLuhan reads it as a kind of embrace carried to mystical heights. The war machine of Virilio and the love machine of McLuhan create quite different kinds of worlds: contest or contact. Further, McLuhan (1964: 52) recognized that the extensions of human beings were auto-amputations born of stress and irritation. Auto-amputations were forms of relief that gave rise to counter-irritants such as numbness and shock, requiring a new sensory equilibrium to be reached. But McLuhan thought that such new ratios would be in their turn achieved and new technological extensions would be embraced and accepted. This implies that human beings serve these extensions or that we are their servomechanisms. But are we servomechanisms of automated deterrence systems? Yes, but what sort of modifications are required to embrace them? According to Virilio, there can be no accommodation (and this applies even after the Cold War in an unstable international enviroment with regard to the proliferation of control over nuclear resources), no new sense ratio. Sure, we are servomechanisms of nuclear weapons systems, but Virilio writes of fear, not of numbness and eventual accommodation.

The nomination of Baudrillard for the position of "French McLuhan" has not resulted in a move to close nominations. The floor was already open, as it were, for nominations well before Kellner and Gane moved their motions, and it remains open, despite critical moves and rhetorical gerrymandering to see that the vote is eventually won, even by default. Before Baudrillard was nominated, the name of Barthes had been put on the floor by journalists in France and Canada. But these cases suggest nothing of the pataphysical effects of reversibility: isn't McLuhan really a Canadian Baudrillard? As absurd as this seems, McLuhan's contemporary return to relevance in the diverse area of new information technologies has a Baudrillardian glow about it, given that he is being updated for a new generation in the largely borrowed, but inflated and exaggerated, conceptual language Baudrillard had put into circulation throughout the 1980s – the time of his most widespread influence in the English-speaking world, to be sure. At times more McLuhan than McLuhan himself and at others anti-McLuhanite to the core, Baudrillard's ambivalence toward McLuhan reveals the limits of the nomination, no matter how it is phrased.

NOTES

1 I develop at length the concept of ambivalence, especially in relation to Baudrillard, in my book *Undisciplined Theory* (London: Sage, 1998). The primary emotion of the between is ambivalence. This is the place and condition of many young theorists in the academy who have not found a discipline in which to settle. They are undisciplined theorists. The task of undisciplined theory in the between is to feel and think its fundamental ambivalence, and to spread instability through ambivalence, with and against the disciplines, and the lip-service paid to interdisciplinarity. The undisciplined theorist "should be," to paraphrase Barthes, "that uninhibited person who shows his/her behind to the Disciplinary Father."

2 Baudrillard's deconstruction of Freud's joke book has been completely overlooked by analysts interested in postmodernism and psychoanalysis. Freud's ideas on wit also inspired Michel de Certeau to think through the tactical relevance of timing and technique involved in lively retorts and colorful invective: what Baudrillard calls "subversion by reversion." It seems to me that Freud elaborated a theory of smut that lacked reciprocity in the supercharged Baudrillardian sense of the concept because dirty talk was always directed at women by men, with the result that the former were supposed to be aroused by the latter's exhibition of their arousal. In a classic psychoanalytic stranglehold, women's resistance, due to "inflexibility," was really a sign of arousal. In Freud's world, women do not talk dirty to men (nor to one another).

6

GALAXIES OF SIMULACRA

In this final chapter I would like to tie together several strands of my presentation. In the previous chapter I noted Baudrillard's borrowing of McLuhan's sense of a gap in historical experience. I want to take up in greater detail McLuhan's opinions about Québec. If, according to McLuhan and Baudrillard, history may be said to have major gaps, the future may, just as strangely, have already happened. Baudrillard's refrain that the year 2000 has already arrived, this pataphysics of the year 2000 which serves as a theoretical perch from which to look back on the end of the millennium, perhaps even of history, and the world, before it arrives, was occupied by McLuhan as well with regard to the threat of Québec's separation from Canada. This is not so much a Canadian preoccupation, although, surely, it is that, too, as it leads into the broader political question of McLuhan's representation of so-called "tribal" cultures and "otherness." While this "alreadyness" is a variant of McLuhan's more general claim that he only predicted things that had already happened, anyway, his characterization of French Canadian culture owes a great deal to his understanding of nationalism and the search for identity in a retribalizing world. So, I will be handling and tying together several strands at once in order to explain how McLuhan runs together related themes, supporting them on the basis of a broad distinction between so-called galaxies. The key texts for my reading are *The Gutenberg Galaxy* (1962) and two interviews: the famous *Playboy* interview (McLuhan 1969g), and the less well-known interview with his French translator Paré in *Forces* magazine (McLuhan 1973a). The Québec question raises the issue of McLuhan's own reading of French Canadian culture as a hippy scene plugged into a technologically generated version of linguistic nationalism. Moreover, the notions of gaps in historical experience and the implosion of the future in the present pose the question of how McLuhan's galaxies of simulacra stand in relation to the numerous triphasic models that one finds in postmodern social theory.

In Canada today McLuhan is on everyone's lips, and so is Québec, but for different reasons. There was a time, however, when the reasons seemed complementary. The heady renaissance of McLuhanism that we are now experiencing, especially on the Internet and in some of the more thoughtful pockets of cyberculture, coexists with the latest expressions and fallout of Québec nationalism. The same two fluxes coexisted in 1967 in the form of McLuhan's launch into francophone consciousness at Expo '67 and Charles de Gaulle's famous "Vive le Québec libre" speech. Everything new is old again.

No one, however, could change the fact that McLuhan openly denied the importance of language for French Canadian nationalism and considered de Gaulle's famous speech to have missed the point. As he concluded in the anonymously written news report on his Expo remarks in *La Presse* (n.a. 1967b):

> poor de Gaulle is even more lost than the rest because he thinks that in recognizing the French language, he can understand French Canadians. This is not the case since he himself is a man of the nineteenth century speaking to hippies.

McLuhan's hippies were "tribal," "feudal," often but not necessarily of a symbolic "Third World" or at least "non-Western," and most certainly cool and implosive. What made such groups all alike was that there was no point, his argument went, for them to Westernize, that is, to modernize, industrialize, to pursue literacy, to develop, then, because in so doing they would leave behind the very things which, for McLuhan, made them perfectly adaptable to the cool configuration of the Global Village: the oral, tactile togetherness of the electrified Western universe of communications. Such "others" were already cool, but they didn't know it. Which is to say, they didn't know themselves, or their self-understanding did not yet include the words of this prophet. This is not very different from Baudrillard's (1986) claim in *Amérique* that Americans, like other "savages," do not understand themselves, and this is what is charming about them. For no good reason whatsoever, except for the sake of its own poetry, McLuhan believed that people of the "Third World" had an immediate encounter with, and unimpeded access to, the latest Western insights and technologies. The least advanced by Western standards were really the most advanced, that is the most prepared for the new technological environments, according to McLuhan's (1962: 27) hypotheses, this made advanced countries "disadvantaged" with regard to such environments. According to Baudrillard's theoretical travelogue, even though Americans live in such a hyperreal country, they are blind to their role as models of simulation. What it means for cool thinkers such as Baudrillard and McLuhan to possess this knowledge may be grasped through the paradoxes they employ in order to generate it.

M(A)CPQ

The 1973 interview with McLuhan conducted by Paré and published in the Hydro-Québec magazine *Forces* explicitly addresses the question of separation and separatist politics. McLuhan's responses are candid and at first glance surprisingly acute; that is, they were "surprisingly" so because McLuhan had a talent for avoiding direct commentaries on such vitally important political matters. What I want to show is how seemingly acute McLuhan's views on Québec were, and how through paradox McLuhan managed to efface them.

Paré:　　You wrote, in 1967, that the separation of French Canada has already occurred.
McLuhan:　Oh yes . . .
Paré:　　And French Canada is still there . . .
McLuhan:　No, it has dropped out [*décroché*].

(McLuhan 1973a: 70)

A break in the action is in order. Paré appears belligerently literal in this exchange, and quite unwilling to let McLuhan deny the obvious. The French translation of this interview, which was conducted in English, renders dropping out as *décroché*; already there is a sense in which McLuhan is going to be let off the hook, as it were (or, perhaps more actively, taken off the hook as one says of a telephone receiver), by his well-placed French lieutenant. Further along, the political tide comes in:

Paré:　　You wrote too that we could even have a civil war if the French Canadians got too obstreperous. Was 1970 that civil war or just a rehearsal?
McLuhan:　You see, the war is on. The war doesn't have to be fought with guns anymore. The war is on and the country has dropped out. But so have a lot of other people dropped out, in other parts of the world too. There are several wars raging at the same time. Every group has its own mafia, and sure the kids are having their wars. French Canada dropped out but no more than in the sense that English Canada also has dropped out of Confederation.

(McLuhan 1973a: 70)

The image of the "dropout" was a favorite of McLuhan's. If you were anyone significant you were dropping out of something (contained or packaged: school or the corporation or Confederation), and tuning into or turning onto the "global electric theater." Why drop out? To tune in, of course, in order to hone one's non-specialized perception and join or make a "mafia" – McLuhan was big on families! Mafias emerge unexpectedly from hierarchized, rigid structures and shape culture by controlling information; clearly, hackers and phreaks and those into the computer virus scene are McLuhanesque mafiosi, as are independent filmmakers (McLuhan and Nevitt 1972). Mafiosi innovate in the ongoing war – fought with "flames" or subpoenas in the case of pirates and cybercops – understood in terms of the displacements effected by new technologies. But McLuhan's approach to the question of separation is clear enough: to drop out is what everybody is doing, and thus, there is nothing very singular about French Canadian nationalist aspirations. English Canada does the same thing. In fact, nationalism is the inevitable aftershock of the revolution in new technologies and the radical changes it brings to human comprehension. This has a ring of truth to it, like any political horoscope, but it reduces history to technology and difference to sameness: *vive la différence* because it is really the same. Difference is a great leveler because it sets terms in specific interrelationships and controls them, ensuring their proximity to one another because any given term's identity is based solely on its relations with other terms in the system. Nationalism clings to the notion of country within given boundaries and a language through which a people may define themselves. This makes nationalist aspirations paradoxical because if they are a result of unifying circuits and systems, they are also at the same time an attempt to defend themselves against the threat of homogenization.

I shall now consider McLuhan's remarks on nationalism in the *Playboy* interview so as to draw out the implications of his view. Leaving aside his "prediction" of the Balkanization of the United States, he is explicit about the consequences of the new media: psychical and sensory integration, but social decentralization, and the development of what he called "tribal ministates." Eventually, he speculated, psychical unity or "tribal bonds" will win out over linguistic, ethnic, religious and/or ideological differences, with the emergence of a "world tribe." This psychic reunification was what made decentralized political entities viable, in McLuhan's estimation. In short, McLuhan's understanding of nationalism was subordinate to his mystical hypothesis about the development of a "global telepathy," a "global consciousness" of the human family living together psychically in peace and harmony, even if they were physically separated.

Let's return, then, to McLuhan's (1973a: 70) interview with Paré (after a discussion of nationalism):

Paré: Do you think that Québec or French Canadian nationalism is maybe a way of getting revenge on the conquerors of 1750?

McLuhan: I hope so. If I were a French Canadian, I would spend most of my energy fighting the bastards who ran the country, who made it English. Yes, I would. I'd be a violent anti-English person if I lived in Québec. But, on the other hand, I can be just as violently anti-English here, I don't have to be in Québec. I have been very anti-English, right here, but the English really have lost everything so it is no longer much fun kicking them in the ass, because they're finished, you know. They have had it. They are the dropouts of our times. But the Americans too are dropping out, their way of life is no longer the real new way of life in the world.

According to McLuhan, one could be anti-English anywhere, and it wouldn't make much difference. To be anti-English is to be obsolete, especially if one is inspired by French Canadian nationalism, which itself clings to the outdated notions of country, language and point of view. The paradox is a virulent form of identification since it turns on a neutralizing regime of definitions. A further implication is that McLuhan would be, as an anti-English Quebecker but not a Québécois, flogging a dropped-out horse, which is to say, he would be just another example of a "pre-industrial" person who didn't understand how contemporary they were because they uncomprehendingly pursued a politics of self-determination based on segmentations such as "English" and "French" and "separation" in general, and did so against the grain of the implosions of space–time with the speed of new media technologies, the rise of a planetary consciousness, and the triumph of pattern recognition over point of view. McLuhan wanted to dictate the desires of other cultures and nations, putting so-called outdated goals such as an industrial infrastructure into their mouths, only to then call them uncomprehending and, by implication, unappreciative of the fact that they had already, unknown to themselves, graduated immediately to the electric technological circus. He uttered this as if in the global political economy outdated products, processes and policies were not forcibly exported to these nations in the maintenance of poverty and various other dependencies (and this even obtains in certain regions of the so-called "developed world").

Separation, like the year 2000, has already taken place. But it happened ever so gently, so no one noticed a thing. As McLuhan specified, nothing is old, everything is new: "there is nothing old under the sun," McLuhan said to Paré. This is an extreme form of proto-Baudrillardian fatalism. Baudrillard adds, standing before the Berlin Wall, before the two hemispheres of Berlin (a nod to McLuhan, to be sure), that "it is impossible to capture the tremor of terror. Everything is insignificant – here, at the pinnacle of history self-exposed by its violence, everything is eerily quiet like an abandoned November field" (Baudrillard 1989: 35). Everyone has dropped out, everyone is indifferent. In these terms, everyone is "frostbitten in advance" before the referendum that keeps the vital organs of social enumeration running long after the political and historical body has passed away. The latest polls report on the condition of a corpse whose keepers stubbornly insist that it remain on public display.

McLuhan was truly fascinated by the liberal politicians of the 1970s such as Pierre Trudeau, Jerry Brown and Valéry Giscard d'Estaing. Indeed, McLuhan became a self-appointed adviser to Trudeau, whose tribalness he likened to the Beatles', even though he did not agree with many of his policies, which he found far too liberal. Trudeau's persona was cool, like television: low-definition and eliciting participation in the completion of its content. Québécois McLuhanites such as Jacques Languirand (1982: 173–75), whose interest was in the participatory nature of magic from Pythagoras to

103

McLuhan, made the connection between the hot/cool distinction and political expediency: if Trudeau was cool, then Jean Drapeau (former Mayor of Montréal) was surely hot, a man of radio in a television era whose definition was too complete and did not invite much participation (ironically, Drapeau was cool enough if one thinks of the massive participation he required of Montréal taxpayers to service the heavy debt incurred by hosting the Olympics in 1976). Languirand was interested in what is now called spin-doctoring: the cooling down of a political image or the reheating of a cool message on the level of style, in both esthetic and semantic terms. In other words, damage control and positive spins through *macluhanisme*.

McLuhan's praise for Trudeau, coupled with his pronouncements about the gaps in Québécois historical experience – perhaps I should say the intervals in the historical experience of a tactile culture revealed by Expo '67 – placed him in the federalist camp in the minds of many politically active Quebeckers aligned with the nationalist movement. But McLuhan was not only identified with federalist politicians: he was also a Catholic. This was a double whammy, for he was not merely politically suspect (a co-conspirator with the oppressor Trudeau, who called the army into the streets of Montréal during the October Crisis of 1970) but also aligned with the church as a dominant conservative institution out of whose shadow progressive elements in Québécois civil society had struggled to emerge. The only one who was really cooler than Trudeau was, after all, Jesus. And the Jesus of Montréal was a McLuhanite. Recall in my introduction that I briefly developed the relationship between religion and technology. More than a few pundits noted the influence of McLuhanite Christians at Expo '67, for instance, referring specifically to his influence on the design of the Christian Pavilion (Cox 1967) and the retrofitting of Jesus as a cool operator, quick with aphorisms, parables, puns and a variety of non-explicit pedagogical tactics, resisting the temptation to speak plainly, to heat up his messages for the sake of the scribes and Pharisees (Matson 1968). Pier Paolo Pasolini may have showed us a Marxist Jesus, but McLuhan and his followers believed in a hippy Jesus. Journalist Tom Wolfe provided a portrait of Jesus as a bohemian in his famous essay on McLuhan "What If He Is Right?" Wolfe (1965) observed:

> McLuhan Temple! McLuhan in church – the Rev. William Glenesk brings McLuhan into the pulpit of his church, Spencer Memorial, on Remson Street in Brooklyn Heights, one week night in a kind of . . . apotheosis of McLuhan cultism. Glenesk is the "hip" Presbyterian minister who has had jazz combos, dancers, sculpture – graven images! – in church. He brought McLuhan in one night and put him in the pulpit and it became . . . cult! Like a melting of all the solitary souls, from the cubicles of the NYU Bronx campus to the lofts of East 10th Street, who had discovered McLuhan on their own.

This is a precursor of the cybercult activities of *Wired* magazine as well as the Gen-X churches of today.

The "philosophical bomb" that was McLuhan, as Maurice Tassart put it in *Carrefour* in 1967, was an example of brilliant pyrotechnics with catastrophic fallout. Still, when Jean Sarrazin, director of *Forces*, wrote to McLuhan explaining that granting this interview would be seen as a gesture of friendship to French Canadian society, it is surprising that he did not seize the opportunity to "clarify" or even modify his most contentious theses on Québec (*MP* 137/1), theses that he had been spouting to the press throughout 1967 on television on shows such as *Telescope*.[1] He did seem to take a sympathetic position by identifying himself in speculative terms with anti-English actions, even violent ones, but turned this into a criticism, even repeating the most damaging claim of all: language didn't matter any more. There was nothing more that Paré, or anyone, could do about that.

Rethinking the conjunction of McLuhan and Québec means setting the proponents of cool media liberalism against the hardline post-Lévesque péquistes and the conservative elements of the Bloc Québécois. Not much has changed since the late 1960s: liberal federalism is trying to recycle itself and péquistes are trying to reterritorialize in an "uncanny" landscape dominated by two former colleagues of the most hated prime minister in the history of Canada in a battle for the hearts and minds of Quebeckers. Whether this reterritorialization can be, to use one of the terms of Félix Guattari and Antonio Negri (1990: 141), placed "among those movements of nationalist territorialization – Basque, Palestinian, Kurdish – which assume, to a certain extent, the great deterritorialized flows of Third World struggles and immigrant proletariats" or "the movements of reactionary nationalist reterritorialization" marked by oppressive and degrading conservatisms is not very difficult to decode: the reactionary and racist conservatism of leading péquiste politicians has been let out of the bag. René Lévesque really is a ghost.

Today, in the time of "renewed" McLuhanism and Liberal federalism in Canada (the latter in the guise of fiscal and social conservatism), and recurring debates about separation and/or sovereignty association, if there is a specter haunting the mediascape it is surely Lévesque. If McLuhan was a prophet of the age of television as such, Lévesque was an *animateur* of the age of Québécois television. He was a driving force behind the internationalization of French Canadian society in the 1950s through CBC public affairs programs such as *Carrefour* (where he worked with Languirand) and *Point de mire*. He was not a theorist of the media, but readily offered his reflections (in – where else? – the pages of *Forces* in 1973) on the relations between information, communications and social and political change, and the refocussing of international reporting onto Québec events. CBC reporter, talking-head, minister in Jean Lesage's Liberal government, and founder of the Mouvement Souveraineté-Association, Lévesque's contributions to media and politics are an antidote of sorts to the theoretical poltergeists of *macluhanisme*. Revisiting the influence of Lévesque is a way to resingularize an otherwise formalistic, abstract and technologically reductionistic definition of media employed by McLuhan and devoid of specific content – except what each user brings to the medium; an approach insensitive to the cultural specificity of language, and outside of the local and provincial histories of catalyzing political events. Yet McLuhan's French lesson remains eerily prescient for an electorate paralyzed by representations of themselves as suffering from referendum fatigue: separation has already taken place, and the only remaining issue is how to pose the question the next time around and, for all intents and purposes, in order to provide the answer of (re)association. And sovereignty, as even the purists realize, becomes more difficult to achieve in a free-trading global economy.

THE "TRIBES" OF THE GLOBAL VILLAGE

The analysis of the tropes of primitivist discourse (Torgovnik 1990) finds an extraordinary wealth of material in the writings of McLuhan. Any reader of *The Gutenberg Galaxy* will have noticed his deployment of a general category called the "tribal," and the enormous amount of work it is made to perform throughout the book. The tribal in McLuhan contains a diversity of cultures, things, experiences and lack of sensory biases; so many things, in fact, that it is difficult to describe without lapsing into a simple inventory of its contents. One way to make the category empty itself is to pose some of Torgovnik's questions to McLuhan. Since McLuhan almost completely eschewed ethno-graphic detail, however, it is not ethnographic representations as such that are so much at issue but, rather, his representation of a diverse selection of nations and cultures as tribal *through* his galactic categories. With McLuhan, then, galaxies replace ethnographic categories, and within these galaxies a series of oppositions (cool/hot; implosive/explosive; linear/mosaic, and the rest) serve as signposts. The focus of these galaxies is the psychic and social implications of sensory (re)organization focussed and brought about by fundamental technological change. I want to show that McLuhan's analysis of globalization is built on a parade of unanalyzed and naively deployed tribal tropes.

While it may be the case that McLuhan, in concert with the major tropes of primitivist discourse, defined the tribal as "different," believing that such societies, if one may call them that, held the key to a universal understanding of human nature, he also closed the gap between them and us in the following way: they are already like we are today, and should not strive to become what we were like yesterday (as I have shown, according to this thinking the seventeenth-century Quebecker is perfectly adapted to the twentieth-century mosaic and, hip, let us say, hippy McLuhanites in Québec who have turned on by dropping out have an affinity with their seventeenth-century predecessors). The tribal is exotic yet familiar, and it is deployed in the search for a universal

106

truth because to know them is to know the most up-to-date parts of ourselves. They may be different; they may be exotic; they may be other in so many ways, but for McLuhan the West is retribalizing, and retribalization, after a long period of Gutenbergian detribalization, is valorized with reference to the adequacy of tribal sensory life in our contemporary technological environment. McLuhan's (1962: 46) premiss of similarity hinges on the "connaturality" of our culture with that of the non-literates, that is, the pre-Gutenbergian tribes. The phases of technologically driven galactic change, from traditional oral societies (non- or pre-literate) through literacy to post-literacy, end as the Global Village goes tribal again since "we have recreated it [non- or pre-literate cultural experience] electronically within our own culture" (1962: 46). Yet McLuhan specified that pre- and post-literate cultures were not identical. Connaturality means similarity on the level of the criteria McLuhan used to describe his galaxies and distinguish between non-literate and literate (I shall return to this).

McLuhan's *The Gutenberg Galaxy* is saturated with the tropes of primitivist discourse. For instance, instead of pre-capitalist, McLuhan's tribes were pre-literate. That is, they were oral and auditory societies living as much at the birth of the West, or even in medieval times, as in modern Russia (an oral, non-literate, auditory society; McLuhan 1962: 20), or in any number of audile-tactile societies such as India; included in this list are the tribal "people of the ear" living in China (and Japan, as well, since neither have phonetic alphabets, McLuhan added; why, then, are French-Canadians so tribal?). Despite their advanced technologies and literacy, the Germans, too, "retained the core of auditory tribal unity"; unidentified nomadic peoples and Eskimos (McLuhan 1962: 66–67) are just as tribal because they are funadamentally non-visual. The list goes on. As one of McLuhan's French readers noted, capturing the ambiguity of this inexact ethnology, "tribal man does not necessarily live in an archaic society; it is his manner of living and thinking which is archaic" (Bourdin 1970: 62). For Bourdin, the tribal man of the Global Village was a sort of hippy, at home in a Happening, or a block party, a free concert in a park, living in a mass-mediated, auditory-tactile, village. The implication is that McLuhan's anthropology is utopian and idealist. In reviewing some of the criticisms of McLuhan's anthropology, Theall (1971: 63–66) observed that his attitude toward primitivism actually underwent a change from the period of *The Mechanical Bride* to *The Gutenberg Galaxy*. The metaphor of the "tribal drum" was in the early 1950s

> one of the great threats to man's sense of discrimination and contem-
> porary civilization. Tribalism, and consequently re-tribalization,
> had from that perspective seemed to require a society which was
> passive and static. During the *Explorations* period, McLuhan met and
> worked closely with Ted Carpenter, an anthropologist interested in
> language, culture, and personality and who was studying Eskimos.

The association led to a growing interest on McLuhan's part in the dimensions of the primitive and to a reassessment of what this primitivism meant.

(Theall 1971: 65)

It was the perception of non-linear patterns that some anthropological research revealed about native cultures as diverse as Aivilik Eskimos and Trobriand Islanders that interested McLuhan.

Elsewhere one reads that, for McLuhan, the tribal, like the primitive, is quintessentially African (Torgovnik 1990: 11), and stereotypically "dark" in the play of light metaphors; indeed, the "return to the Africa within" (McLuhan 1962: 45, 255) that is vital to McLuhan's sense of the affinity of the contemporary with the pre-literate renders Africa psychical. This sort of claim is common enough today in McLuhanatic cyberbabble; witness pop electronic music composer Brian Eno's (1995: 204) recent appearance on the cover of *Wired* magazine and his claim that both nerds and computers do not have enough Africa in them, which is to say that the "return" was interrupted by the bad hangover of literacy.

Further, the tribal is applied just as easily to subordinate groups in the West, including but not limited to McLuhan's favorite examples, African and Native Americans, upon whose "cultural advantages" he dwelled in the *Playboy* interview. McLuhan believed that racism was explicable as a kind of subliminal jealousy that whites felt in the face of the obvious "psychical and social superiority" of these tribal peoples. He voiced, to be fair, concerns about the consequences of rivalries between Black and the dominant white culture, and the latter's extermination of the former. But his diagnosis was reactionary: African Americans are sorely mistaken if they think that they can make progress by entering the "senescent" mechanical, literate world. The "backward is really superior" thesis was nothing less than a policy of repression completely lacking a political economic analysis of American racism and an acknowledgment, in any specific – embodied or historically situated – way whatsoever, of the history of slavery and the systematic eradication of Native Americans; certainly, McLuhan (1969g: 69) recognized and explicitly stated that

the Negro and Indian seem to always get a bad deal; they suffered first because they were tribal men in a mechanical world, and now as they try to detribalize and structure themselves within the values of the mechanical culture, they find the gulf between them and a suddenly retribalizing society widening rather than narrowing.

These tribal peoples are doomed, according to McLuhan, and even worse, in speaking for them, he can demonstrate how little they understand of the contemporary world as he defined it, making of their desires for literacy in the broadest possible sense a mistaken "lemming leap," as it put it. There are two serious matters at issue here. The first is this typically racist animal metaphor that McLuhan trotted out in the *Playboy* interview and used not only to strip African and Native Americans of intelligence but also seal their fate to the extent that certain species of lemmings have been observed undertaking a suicidal migration to the sea. The implication of McLuhan's animalization of African and Native Americans was that they set themselves on a suicidal journey. In the gloom of these notions McLuhan's afterthought that all the tribes would eventually overcome their differences was sheer mysticism and a bad prediction. The second issue is the uncritical use of literacy, which is nothing less than inflammatory when taken in the context of the history and practice of slavery in the United States. There is nothing in McLuhan about the role played by the denial of education to slaves, and their largely secretive struggles to learn how to read and write, as an important project toward freedom rather than a step away from it.

In another way, however, these sorts of matters served McLuhan as a substitute for the tired evolutionist premiss of primitivist discourse: they are what we were; therefore, to document them is to understand how we came to be the way that we are today. For McLuhan, instead, tribal others need to be studied so that we can better understand ourselves and in so doing retribalize ourselves by going, metaphorically, backward, thinking in a more non-linear way, becoming more like them in terms of a change in sensory orientation and consciousness, shifting from the part or fragment to the whole. Despite the best efforts of critics such as Jonathan Miller (1971: 46) to hang McLuhan out to dry on the basis of his promotion of the "impudent myth of Southern egalitarianism," McLuhan's brand of racism – a word Miller mentions but in a negative construction – "I do not mean to suggest that McLuhan is a racist" – was a direct consequence of the backfiring of his galactic categories. There is, in addition, a certain amount of stereotyping in McLuhan that leaves itself open to ridicule, such as his refrain in *The Gutenberg Galaxy* and elsewhere that an audile-tactile culture resonates with the sounds of "tribal drums," which sounds a bit like a typical case of New Age cultural appropriation designed for vacationing executives, which was not far from the truth given McLuhan's penchant for hawking his intellectual wares in the boardrooms of America and abroad.

Before I consider the place of McLuhan's galaxies in relation to models of historical change found in postmodern social theory, two points remain to be discussed. The first is that both McLuhan and Baudrillard approve of the harshness of the tribal and symbolic, respectively. For McLuhan, permissiveness (sex and drugs) was a phenomenon of overlapping galaxies; but when retribalization is realized, restrictiveness will reign (family values and austerity measures). Similarly, Baudrillard considered the symbolic order to be brutally hierarchical; his version of the tribal is a cruel society, and the rules governing it are inflexible and restrictive. This is Baudrillard's anti-democratic, pre-simulacral world in which the reference of symbols (motivated signs) is sure and strictly limited, obligatory, as he puts it. Baudrillard's theory of symbolic exchange leads one to the conclusion that his project is to recreate a symbolic order in contemporary society. It is difficult to avoid drawing such a conclusion, but it is wrong to do so, Baudrillard (1992: 296) maintains. Despite his considerable debts to Marcel Mauss and the noble socialist sentiment of adapting societies of the gift (primarily Melanesian and AmerIndian societies as they are represented in Western and social anthropological ethnographies) to his own society (i.e. French society of the 1920s), Baudrillard parts company with Mauss in stating "we cannot recreate a symbolic order." Baudrillard's revolutionary anthropology is, to make a long story short, not very anthropological, and its radicalism is purely theoretical, not to mention paradoxical. It is a striking hybrid of fieldwork from the 1960s among the Sara in Chad and proselytizing by psychoanalytic missionaries in Senegal (see Genosko 1998). With Baudrillard there can be no retribalization; only its theorization is possible. It is interesting to note that Lyotard's (1993: 106) criticism of Baudrillard's anthropology is founded on his uncritical inheritance of "ethnology's good savage" and the fantasy of a non-alienated, non-productive precapitalist society existing sometime and somewhere. These savages may as well have been good hippies or nomads of consumer culture.

The second point requires the gathering together of the key terms of McLuhan's distinction between the pre- or non-literate and the literate worlds, that is, between the tribal and typographic peoples, as a point of clarification. The sensory life of psychically tribal peoples is audile-tactile, involving the interplay of the senses, while linear-thinking literate persons are, sensorially speaking, highly specialized, visual and pictorial. In temporal terms, McLuhan tells us that the former were oriented toward the simultaneous and the latter were stuck on the sequential; while spatially, McLuhan's tribes were supposedly nomadic, and the typographic (wo)men, sedentary, the former existed in a sacred, magical space, and the latter occupied a profane, mechanical and rational world.

Deleuze and Guattari (1977: 557, n. 56) acknowledge their debt to anthropologist Edmund ("Ted") Carpenter's work on Eskimo culture, and hence the influence of the McLuhan milieu given Carpenter's close work with him on the journal *Explorations*, for instance, in which the Eskimo book they cite appeared as a special issue (no. 9, 1959). Deleuze and Guattari engage in a McLuhanesque space studies in their discussions of smooth haptic spaces and striated, visual spaces, those of nomads and sedentary peoples, respectively, bringing into focus and enriching the distinctions McLuhan learned to appreciate from Carpenter (especially the idea that the Eskimo was fundamentally a non-visual person; McLuhan 1962: 66–67). Smooth, nomadic, rhizomatic space is heterogeneous, while striated, centered, tree-like space is homogeneous. Haptic space in Deleuze and Guattari and McLuhan, following

Carpenter, is marked by the variability of directions and acenteredness, and its tactile contacts also make it implosive. Carpenter (1966: 59) writes: "Entire Eskimo societies are implosive: everybody is involved with everybody simultaneously and instantaneously. There is no isolating 'individualism' and no emphasis upon isolation of sight from other senses." Deleuze and Guattari (1977: 494) make the same point about what Carpenter called "ice space":

> Where there is close vision, space is not visual, or rather the eye itself has a haptic, nonoptical function: no line separates earth from sky, which are of the same substance; there is neither horizon nor background nor perspective nor limit nor outline nor form nor center; there is no intermediary distance, or all distance is intermediary. Like Eskimo space.

Carpenter's Eskimo is also a Deleuzoguattarian (wo)man of lines rather than points; lacking both a view and a point, s/he is in flux, without form, the perfect collective assemblage for a nomadology adapted to the Global Village and free of the disciplinary demands of anthropology. Let there be no doubt about it: close vision is perfectly adapted to the television screen.

THREE STRIKES AND YOU'RE POSTMODERN

As a social theory postmodernism has recourse to triphasic models with one foot in the economic and the other in the semiotic. Following Jameson, postmodernity is the hyperspace of multinational capital in a late form – not post-capitalism, but an intensified capitalism that has no trouble accommodating the sort of globalism "predicted" by McLuhan. The description of this intense phase requires the integration of both economic and semiotic categories. Models of the mutations of capitalism borrowed from Marx's *The Poverty of Philosophy* (1936) and Ernest Mandel's *Late Capitalism* (1978) provide the economic backbone of postmodern theory and guide the effort to describe the waning of use-value and the rise of information and representation as commodities. Representation in postmodernity is a commodity produced and consumed alongside a staggering array of cultural forms that are direct expressions of economic activity. At the extreme, everything in social life becomes cultural and a commodity; the cultural and the economic become one, since the cultural is no longer a veil hiding and distorting economic reality.

Marx and Mandel describe in closely related ways the generalization of exchange-value and the expansion of capital. On the one hand, the transition from feudal society and the dominance of use-value over exchange-value, as well as the availability of small surpluses for marketplace exchanges, to

111

industrial production in which everything produced is exchangeable as a commodity, culminates in consumer capitalism and its "general corruption" of even the most abstract qualities. On the other hand, market capitalism witnesses the industrial-driven growth of national markets, and mutates into monopoly capitalism with imperially driven market expansions into colonized states; recently, the asymmetrical articulations of colonialism have given way to a multinational capitalism marked by the transnational flows of capital expanding, one may say, endo-colonially, pre-eminently into the logic of representation itself, as well as globally into hitherto untapped domains.

Jameson's version of these phases is best described as the bastardization of referentiality by reification. At the dawn of capitalism signs referred unproblematically to their referents. This reifying literality apparently destroyed an earlier, pre-capitalist, so-called "magical language" (Jameson 1991:96). Reification is the key force for it is nothing less in Jameson's mind than that of the logic of capital. The "ruthless separation and disjunction, of specialization and rationalization" that the "corrosive force" of reification worked by means of literality then turned on reference itself. This is the moment of modernism in which language withdraws into its own house, away from the referent and the real. Reification does not destroy reference; rather, it enfeebles it by disjoining the sign from its referent in the structural interrelations of signifiers which produce the effect of meaning in the signified. Yet the distance of signs from things and the "autonomy of culture" is a paradoxical strength of modernism, for what affords critical distance also entails "a certain otherworldly futility," Jameson astutely observes (1991: 96). Reification continues unabated, and this time, in the postmodern scene, its disjunctivity invades the sign and cleaves the signifier from the signified, isolating signifier from signifier; even a weakened referentiality disappears altogether, as meaning itself, in the form of the signified, is eclipsed by the pure play of signifiers. This is Jameson's version of schizophrenia as the postmodern condition. Literality returns in the vividness of the signifier isolated from interrelationships which give it meaning in the hell of a perpetual present (Jameson 1983: 120).

Jameson's debts to Baudrillard will be obvious to anyone who recalls my overview of the orders of simulacra. The mutations of the law of value from the natural, through the market, to the structural, is paralleled by the transition from the dominant forms of the counterfeit, production and simulation. Jameson's fantasy of a "magical language" has its parallel in Baudrillard's dream of a pre-semiotic world of symbolic exchange that has been corrupted by semiology. The modern sign is born with the semiological corruption of the symbol by arbitrariness and the withdrawal of reference, which was once sure and cruel. This corruption is also an emancipation of sorts from the obligation of reference. The countergift retains a certain amount of charm for Baudrillard because it is not very far removed from an anthropological fantasy of pre-semiotic, concrete interpersonal relations governed by gift exchange (obligation and reciprocity).

The simplest mechanistic expression of this level would be the automaton, since it is a theatrical counterfeit of human being that plays with appearances by analogy. In the second order the charm of the masquerade disappears with industrial production, seriality and mechanistic operationalization. The trade in appearances is lost to the production of equivalents: the serial repetition of the same in the dull, crude and technical mass production of objects. This is exemplified by the robot that does not play, either with appearances or with analogy, but is simply, and in the technical terms that dominate it, supposed to be the equivalent of the human. The robot does not play; rather, it works. In the third order of simulacra the code and generative models reign over all semiosis. Mechanical reproduction is transcended by the emanation of all values from the system (code or model), from which it follows that the real is conceived of in terms of its very reproducibility. The android fits this order quite well since it is generated from a model according to modulated differences. The android is like a robot in the sense that it is the equivalent of a human, but it is of a higher order: it is organic and plays with analogy. While in Jameson literalness plays a role in both the first and third phases, Baudrillard situates the ability to play with analogy and masquerade in both phases as well; in both descriptions, literalness and masquerade indicate the distance from the real and the abstractness of the third phase. Key elements from the first phase recur in the higher-order convulsions that have taken place in the decisive shift from the second to the third phase (for instance, the rise of representation as a commodity and the political economy of sign, in which all that is material melts into signification).

Both Jameson and Baudrillard agree that reification, the concept developed by Hungarian Marxist theorist Georg Lukács in his important book *History and Class Consciousness* (1971) on the basis of Marx's analysis of commodity relations, specifically commodity fetishism, is indispensable for an understanding of the postmodern condition. Baudrillard (1975: 121) is much more cynically attached to the concept than is Jameson, praising it as the only viable critical advance in Marxist thinking capable of rising to the challenge of his diagnosis of the passage from the commodity to the sign form in the third order of simulation. Arguably, the most stirring pages of Jameson's (1991: 313–18) monumental *Postmodernism, or The Cultural Logic of Late Capitalism* are those devoted explicitly to reification. Jameson flags the standard meaning of the term as the demand of capitalism to treat human labor power as a thing, a quantity, a commodity. It is in the disproportion between the wage granted to the worker for his/her labor and the value it produces in goods for the capitalist, that is, the surplus value or profit, that reification stirs: capitalist ideology makes profit appear as a property inherent in goods, a "natural" thing-fetish (this is most powerfully expressed, Lukács (1971:93–94) believed, in Marx's description of interest-bearing capital generating value in itself in the form of interest: a bit like the Baudrillardian signifier whose sole referents are other signifiers). Labor power is sold as if it were a thing outside oneself, and the worker is additionally separated from the product of his/her labor; and the value produced is exchanged as a thing, completely fulfilling the dehumanizing force of capitalist reification. Jameson emphasizes the "effacement" of the production process and the separation between producers and consumers. Reification is essential to consumerism because in Jameson's estimation it silences the voices in one's head that would otherwise wonder about the conditions under which the precious things with which one surrounds oneself were produced. Reification is in this sense "functional" for consumer culture. More radically, however, Jameson (1991: 315) thinks that reification "perpetuat[es] a deep conviction within the consumer that the production of the product in question – attributable no doubt to other human beings in the generic sense – is nonetheless beyond anything you can imagine." The consequence is "a Promethean inferiority complex" (impotence before production, the compensatory titillations of consumerism, the death of the imagination before products themselves) in the face of a completely reified culture. It follows for Jameson that post-modernism is something of a "relief" from the alienations of modernism (the cult of genius, specialism), even if the subsequent invitation to play and produce has its own limitations (for instance, the loss of key modernist categories).

There are, however, several elements from Lukács's analysis that Jameson omits, but which Baudrillard seizes upon without, as is his custom, guiding his readers through the argument. Although Baudrillard considered Lukács's analysis of the concept of reification to be "the only" theoretical development of any note in Marxism, including the work of the Situationists, he still rejected the base upon which Lukács worked; that the commodity form is the "universal category" dominating society. Baudrillard maintains (1975: 121–22) the decisive passage from the commodity form to the sign form reveals a kind of control "more subtle and totalitarian than exploitation" and that, in comparison, the hegemony of the code makes the "quantitative mystery of surplus value appear inoffensive." Lukács's discussion of reification relies on Marx's analysis of the generalization of the commodity form through the worker's self-objectification, the alienation of him/herself from him/herself, based upon the understanding that one's labor-power is seen as something one owns and which may be "disposed of."

But Baudrillard thinks that the generalization of the sign form takes place through the process by which the code controls the production of meaning and difference through a "structural manipulation" that is irreducible to a conscious referential psychology of the use of signs for social differentiation, which is to say, for the sake of a lived distinction. Meaning rather than labor power is at the base of Baudrillard's argument. Reading Baudrillard one cannot fail to be struck that in his brave substitutions and putative advances on Marxian analyses, he has retained some of the most pertinent principles of the theorization of reification. This is especially obvious in his descriptions of the predicament in which one finds oneself when metaphorically facing the code: "whatever one does, one can only respond to the system in its own terms, according to its own rules, answering it with its own signs" (Baudrillard 1975: 127). This is what Lukács called the "contemplative attitude" taken toward one's reified faculties. Activity gives way to contemplation and no attempt is made to transcend the commodity structure because it appears to the reified mind to be "the form in which its own authentic immediacy becomes manifest" (Lukács 1971: 93). This is truly the mirror of servitude held out by capitalism; one is fully integrated into, as Lukács observed, a "perfectly closed system" operating autonomously; in other words, the code. Indeed, where Lukács saw the consequences of the division of labor through rationalization and calculation, Baudrillard read the operationalization of binarity and digitality under the dictates of the structural differentiations of the code.

Where is McLuhan in all of this? Isn't the reification of both physical and psychical faculties perfectly described by his hypothesis of the outering or extension of the human sensorium? Isn't it possible to read McLuhan from beginning to end as an apologist for the contemplative attitude before the whirlpool of commerce? Reification was an amusement that McLuhan did nothing except "scientifically deepen" (the laws of the market are those of the media, as it were), to borrow Lukács's idea of the objective side of reification: the discovery and even the deployment but never the modification of the laws governing the world of commodities. Imagine for a moment that Lukács was referring to the mediascape when he argued that the predicament of life in a capitalist society could be expressed in terms of the human being's confrontation with a reality s/he has made but which is alien to her/him, to such a degree that one is nothing but the object of events, the object of the mediatic message which works one over completely: the medium is the massage. Reaction replaces action. McLuhan's insight into what he called the active "environments" created by new media, whose invisibility and pervasiveness were not easily perceived, is a central and pernicious mystification of capitalism, since the laws governing the society appear as an alien, non-human universe operating autonomously on the basis of "invisible forces that generate their own power" (Lukács 1971: 87).

McLuhan was, then, a perfect example of Lukács's contemplative, bourgeois man. As Kroker once observed, McLuhan lacked a political economy of technology; put more strongly, he completely divorced reification from its economic base; thus, as Lukács (1971: 94–95) would have it, his surface descriptions of the phenomena of reification, and asides about their "painfulness," did nothing but deepen their dehumanizing effects.

For Baudrillard, Marx and Marxist analysts have proved themselves to be incapable of grasping the decisive mutation between the second and third orders of simulacra because of their transfer of principles of analysis from the former to the latter without acknowedging the metaphorization of these principles (Baudrillard 1975: 120). Similarly, McLuhan (1970b) maintained that Marx was stuck on certain principles of analysis (these were, of course, commodities, labor, mode of production, exploitation and profit) and was blind to the "environmental effects" of new products. In other words, for both McLuhan and Baudrillard, Marx's categories were too deeply imbedded in political economy and therefore inadequate for describing contemporary capitalist societies. McLuhan quickly undermined his not particularly well-formed criticisms with a social and political blindness staggering in its implications. McLuhan's habit was, for instance, to criticize Marx and communism for the sake of the ideological obfuscation that new electric service environments are free for all, that communism exists today as an effect of wealth, as if wealth were fairly distributed. Of course, McLuhan's (1968c: 6) "commune-ist form" was a variant of his electric tribalism, which was more tribal than any previously known tribalism: hypertribal. This was the tribalism of films such as Mike Nichols's *The Graduate* (re-released after 30 years) which McLuhan read as an Oedipal drama; and why not, the high-rise apartment was for him a "tribal slum . . . whose effects are uncomfortable but not bad in themselves" (McLuhan 1969h: 2–3); just as the miniskirt was an involving tribal costume marking off the wearer from the establishment, rather than situating women in a particular relation to the establishment.

The "tribes" of McLuhan's traditional age belonged as much to the Greek oral tradition as perhaps any cool, speaking-hearing nexus; vertical suburb, slum or whatever. A key figure is Socrates since he did not write; but Jesus, too, since he was cool; and, of course, Francophone hippies, Blacks and Native Americans, Eskimos, Russians, etc. As far as galaxies go, this one lasted all the way to the fifteenth century when the age of literacy and typographic man was born with the invention of the printing press. Triphasic models have in common a certain vagueness about phases, such as one finds in Baudrillard's simulacra-focussed distinction between the Renaissance, the Industrial Revolution and the post-industrial era, even though the objects marking the transitions are often explicitly flagged (for McLuhan reading and writing undergo significant changes when manuscript culture confronts the printing press; with Baudrillard the theatricality of stucco passes into mechanical means of reproduction or, in other words, substances and forms are displaced by relations and structures (Baudrillard 1993: 53)). Manuscript culture was forever transformed with the mechanical means of reproduction, that is, movable type. It was not until the 1960s that the cool, implosive, electric age emerged and young people began retribalizing with new means. For McLuhan, television was the great "commune-ist" form. Reading McLuhan on Marx is a little like reading Ronald Reagan on Marx. In both cases the discussions employ a few guy-ropes based on borrowed concepts, but remain, for the most part, content to float wherever their own currents take them.

NOTE

1 I consulted a transcript of this Canadian Broadcasting Corporation television program in Box 2, Folder 1 (Mss. 20) in the Shelagh Lindsey Collection, University of Manitoba Archives, Winnipeg.

CONCLUSION

Let's consider a few areas in which further work on McLuhan's French reception may be undertaken on the basis of the groundwork laid by the themes discussed thus far in this book.

Translating McLuhan into French was not an easy task, especially since a translator often had to work in concert with a designer in order to ensure that the concrete aspects of the texts were not lost. One may think of Gilles Robert, for instance, as a kind of French Harley Parker. Robert's company adapted Parker's design of *Counterblast* to suit Paré's translation, all the while grappling with word-objects of a text whose letters lent themselves in different ways in French to iconic expressions of, for example, how "a chair outers the human posterior" (McLuhan 1970a: 39; McLuhan 1972a: 39).

La chaise prolonge
le postérieur.

A chair outers
the human posterior.

The difference between *bum* and *cul* called for ingenious postural correctives. Translation became a kind of chiropractic: with the loss of the iconic elements of the letter "B," the u-shaped seat, and m-shaped chair supports, new conventions were required for "outering" a seated, spreading behind. But *cul* is no derrière, a spreading bottom. The number of letters remained conveniently the same – despite Robert's need to repeat c-u-l in the shape of a shoulder, arm and breast (or is it a nose?) – but *cul* is laden with off-color shades of meaning which lay bare the vulgar "piece of ass" (and a gendered leg) at issue in a profile rather than from a legless behind. The inverted "u" does not so much "outer" the posterior as place it on a pedestal;

118

and not so much of the posterior is outered! But *cul* accomplishes what bum could not, and does so by adding a layer of proprietary sexualization. The inclusion of the leg through the arrangement of "l" looks forward to McLuhan's point that the outering of the posterior involved in the chair led directly to the development of the table, under which one's legs must be made to fit.

The general point is that translating McLuhan into French was a multidimensional undertaking, the study of which helps one to understand how his texts were of necessity reinvented on several semiotic planes; it is especially important to note how the translation gendered the image, enabling the word-object to objectify women's bodies. But imagine, for a moment, what this process of translation would have entailed in other languages (Japanese, etc.).

The confusion and controversy surrounding the translation of *From Cliché to Archetype* (with Watson 1970 and in translation 1973) reveals another facet of the transformation of McLuhan's texts for French readers. The journalist Dumur (1972: 37) reported in *Le Nouvel Observateur* that McLuhan "is preparing to publish a commentary on *Dictionnaire des idées reçues* that he will sign Gustave Flaubert and Marshall MacLuhan." When the work appeared the following year with the title *Du cliché à l'archétype: La foire du sens*. Accompagné du Dictionnaire des idées reçues de Gustave Flaubert, McLuhan's scandalous advance publicity was tempered by the exigencies of publishing and authorship; that is, McLuhan's co-author Wilfred Watson may have disappeared from the cover, but Flaubert did not take his place. It was the translator de Kerckhove who turned *From Cliché to Archetype* into a quasi-symbolist masterpiece.

The translation was immediately met, however, with criticism. Writing in *Le Devoir*, Gilles Marcotte (1974: 17) commented on the translator that: "He has cut here, and added there; replaced quotations from English authors with quotations from French authors (Montaigne, Racine, Blanchot, etc.), which are not always solidly anchored to the text – but, neither are those of McLuhan." Marcotte concluded that de Kerckhove's version was less well developed than McLuhan's original. While McLuhan and de Kerckhove received support for the translation from a variety of quarters, in 1976 McLuhan was still defending de Kerckhove's work in an unpublished letter to Gertrude Le Moyne at *La Presse* (MP 22/20).

Consider this rewriting of the text in the following terms which revisit my discussion of "happenings." In the original English version, McLuhan and Watson emphasized, following analyses of Happenings by several prominent intellectuals such as Susan Sontag, the non-verbal matrix (visual and temporal frames) of such events, the inclusion of an active audience in the proceedings, and the manipulation and radical juxtapositions of everyday environments in the clash of clichés borrowed from different media. Although McLuhan and Watson resisted certain elements of Sontag's definition, such as the tendency of Happenings to use persons as material objects rather than as characters, Sontag's ideas were the main board from which McLuhan and Watson sprang. Read in conjunction with de Kerckhove's sanctioned rewriting, especially the section on "Théâtre," the English text must have served as a kind of Happening for the translator. First, McLuhan's book was not initially rewritten in English before it was translated into French. De Kerckhove's "exploratory and probe functions" – to use McLuhan's terminology – led him to erase numerous references and import new examples to give content and context to McLuhan's concepts for a culturally different readership. Second, de Kerckhove cannot be said to have failed to provide a literal translation; nor did he arbitrarily substitute French for English quotations. Watson, it is evident, did not participate in the rewriting. De Kerckhove's process of rewriting was intensely participatory – even in the banal sense of the working meetings he had with McLuhan over the course of the translation. It is equally participatory for the reader attuned to issues surrounding the translation and French reception of McLuhan's writings. The text is a mosaic of the close translation of selected paragraphs; the exclusion of references to and quotations by such notables as Joyce, Coleridge, Paul Goodman, Chaucer and Charlie Chaplin; bold substitutions which did not miss the point (Baudelaire for Blake); wild media mixes that must have delighted McLuhan (substituting experiments with sound technologies for newspapers); the insertion of current events familiar to French readers (an Italian troupe's performance of *Orlando Furioso* at Les Halles in 1970 – the only Happening cited in either text); and the insertion of details merely suggested in the original (i.e., the names of the Fellini films McLuhan was thinking about at the time but did not name). All of these examples are drawn from only a few pages of the book! *Du cliché à l'archétype* was remade by de Kerckhove in a complex way that included many of McLuhan's own "new" examples in what was considered by both of them to be the superior edition that used Flaubert's definitions as a readymade framework. This remaking did not put de Kerckhove on the list of those nominated for the position of "French McLuhan."

These few considerations clear the way for a more detailed analysis of the translation and reinvention of McLuhan for French and other audiences; the belief (see *MP* 20/81) that certain of his books (*Through the Vanishing Point*) were simply, according to his publishers, too difficult to translate, should not be neglected. In addition, such integral questions of translation turn back toward the study of the claims made on his work from all quarters, especially by groups whose concerns and adaptations were, in some instances, quite mysterious.

The popular French journal *Planète* was launched by Louis Pauwels in 1961. The editorial committee included his close colleague Jacques Bergier, with whom he wrote *Le matin des magiciens* (1960). Pauwels was born in Paris in 1920. His work as a journalist involved him in *Carrefour*, *Figaro Littéraire* and *Combat* (which he edited from 1949 to 1955). He is currently the director of *Figaro Magazine*. He is best known for his esoteric theorizing and novels of fantastic realism, which include a wide range of themes from eastern religions and exorcism to alchemy and secret societies. He is a connoisseur of the paranormal, perhaps even the paranoid. For his part, Bergier may be counted among "non-conformist scientific popularizers" and "science fiction propagandists" in France whose mainstream interests (translating American scientific texts into French) and editorial positions (as the "house intellectual" for the journal *Fiction*) gave way to an overriding interest in the occult and the development, in *Le matin des magiciens* and *Planète*, of "the first French ideology of science fiction" (Ory 1991: 107). In the late 1960s (Thomas 1968; Veyrac 1969), McLuhan took his rightful place alongside the free-spirited futurologists, psychedelic artists, astrologists, wild urbanists and counter-cultural figures of all sorts favored by *Planète*. Once again, McLuhan as visionary was embraced by cultural *animateurs* – who, incidentally, eventually came to package alternative experiences for sale as seminars and vacations – committed to the expression of interdisciplinary knowledges excluded from the magisterial discourses watched over by the professors and other keepers of so-called "closed systems" of thought.

There is an image, however, which captures the lingering resentment over McLuhan's French revolution. On May 8, 1974, *Le Monde* carried a full-page advertisement for La Presse Quotidienne Régionale, in which an angry Gutenberg gave his response to McLuhan's claim that we have left his galaxy of the printed word for the electric media of Marconi. The figure of Gutenberg gave McLuhan what is known informally as the "Italian salute"! Less a response in French than a response by the French, this rather rude gesture of ill-will came from the newspaper sector in the heat of its struggle against television and its perceived demiurge: MacLuhan. Still, as I have argued, MacLuhan was hard to hit, even with hard-hitting advertorial content. His very indistinctness perhaps accounts, in some measure, for his user- and seeker-friendliness.

My exploration of the complex relationship between McLuhan and Baudrillard emphasized the concepts of massage and semiurgy, implosion, participation, and the vicissitudes of the phrase "the medium is the message." In several interviews Baudrillard has readily acknowledged his debt to McLuhan and has stated his basic agreement with the latter's analysis of the media, especially television. Baudrillard inverts, however, McLuhan's sense of a Global Village overflowing with information, access to which increases liberty (Baudrillard 1984b). Baudrillard's inversion takes this course. There is no shared code, he believes, between media senders and mass receivers; there is neither a village atmosphere nor any "right to reply," since the Baudrillardian problematic is focussed on the theorization of symbolically effective forms of response. Baudrillard does not valorize communicative contact. He understands McLuhan's sense of tactility, a somewhat cryptic notion carried forward by de Kerckhove (1991: 47) and others through speculation about sub-muscular responses as the "deep effects" of television, as nothing more than "communication-contact . . . [in] which there is a kind of short-circuit between sender and receiver" (Baudrillard 1996: 166). At the level of the individual, Baudrillard notes, information overload and communicative saturation create a short-circuit described as a "tactile ambience," a generalized, undifferentiated environment of telephasis.

Baudrillard still, on occasion, holds out the possibility that there is some way of mastering implosion and in this sense may be said to flirt with McLuhan's optimism, even if surfing the "tactile ambience" of media culture means that the mass created by media technologies is a neutralizing, implosive energy rather than a positive, expansive explosion. Baudrillard retains the notion of mass in his remarks on media against current trends in communication theory to investigate the conditions of "post-(mass)media" and "multimedia" environments. But he aligns advanced media technologies with indetermination and indifferentiation, to which the mass form, his spongy referent, responds in kind with indifference. The orgy really is over.

McLuhan masters implosion through creative involvement buoyed by religious optimism, downplaying the deleterious effects of technological change, while Baudrillard wallows in a pessimism produced by the effects of simulation, while refusing to relinquish the somewhat mystical hope of a radical anthropological antidote. For both thinkers, implosion is a subtractive form in which loss (whether of space and time or meaning and the social) is regained but in different ways: for McLuhan, in a global community, the development of whose means of involvement remains unchecked; and, for Baudrillard, in an involving, controlled, centripetal collapse which is threatened by a catastrophic explosion. Regardless of these differences, implosion is inevitable and the failure intellectually to master it is the straight gate to irrelevance for any media theorist.

REFERENCES

Alcoun, André *et al.* (1986) *Le pouvoir des médias: mélanges offerts à Jean Cazeneuve*, Paris: Presses Universitaires de France.

Alexandre, Michel (1967) "Marshall McLuhan fumiste ou précurseur?" *Sept-jours* 44 (July 15): 6–8.

d'Arcy, Jean (1974) "Un nouveau medium," *Communications* 21: 9–20.

Babin, Pierre and Iannone, M. (1986) *L'ère de la communication: Réflexion chrétienne*, Paris: Editions du Centurion.

—— —— (1991) *The New Era in Religious Education*, David Smith (trans.), Minneapolis: Fortress Press.

Balle, Francis (1972) *Pour comprendre les médias: MacLuhan*, Paris: Hatier.

Barthes, Roland (1954) *Michelet par lui-même*, Paris: Editions du Seuil.

—— (1957) *Mythologies*, Paris: Editions du Seuil.

—— (1964) "Eléments de sémiologie," *Communications* 4: 91–144.

—— (1966) *Critique et vérité*, Paris: Editions du Seuil.

—— (1967) *Système de la mode*, Paris: Editions du Seuil.

—— (1970) *S/Z*, Paris: Editions du Seuil.

—— (1971) "Changer l'objet lui-même," *Esprit* (April): 613–16.

—— (1975) *Roland Barthes par Roland Barthes*, Paris: Editions du Seuil.

—— (1979) "Lecture in Inauguration of the Chair in Literary Semiology, Collège de France, Jan. 7, 1977," Richard Howard (trans.), *October* 8: 3–16.

Baudrillard, Jean (1967) "Marshall MacLuhan, *Understanding Media: The Extensions of Man*" (review), *L'homme et la société* 5: 227–30.

—— (1968) *Le système des objets*, Paris: Gallimard.

—— (1970) *La société de consommation*, Paris: SGPP.

—— (1972) *Pour une critique de l'économie politique du signe*, Paris: Gallimard.

—— (1973) *Le miroir de la production*, Tournai: Casterman.

—— (1975) *The Mirror of Production*, Mark Poster (trans.), St. Louis: Telos.

—— (1976) *L'échange symbolique et la mort*, Paris: Gallimard.

—— (1978a) *A l'ombre des majorités silencieuses ou la fin du social*, Fontenay-sous-Bois: Cahiers d'Utopie.

—— (1978b) *L'ange de stuc*, Paris: Galilée.

—— (1981a) *For a Critique of the Political Economy of the Sign*, Charles Levin (trans.), St. Louis: Telos.

—— (1981b) *Simulacres et simulations*, Paris: Galilée.

REFERENCES

—— (1983) "Les séductions de Baudrillard," Patrice Bollon (interview), *Magazine littéraire* 193 (March): 80–81.
—— (1984a) "Jean Baudrillard," Christian Deschamps (interview), *Entretiens avec Le Monde 3. Idées contemporaines*, Paris: Editions la Découverte.
—— (1984b) "Game with Vestiges," Salvatore Mele and Mark Titmarsh (interview) and Ross Gibson and Paul Patton (trans.), *On the Beach* 5 (Winter): 19–25.
—— (1986) *Amérique*, Paris: Grasset.
—— (1987) *L'autre par lui-même*, Paris: Galilée.
—— (1988a) *Xerox and Infinity*, Agitac (trans.), London: Touchepas.
—— (1988b) *America*, Chris Turner (trans.), London: Verso.
—— (1989) "The Anorexic Ruins," in *Looking Back on the End of the World*, D. Kamper and C. Wolf (eds.), New York: Semiotext(e).
—— (1990a) *Seduction*, Brian Singer (trans.), Montréal: New World Perspectives.
—— (1990b) *La transparence du mal*, Paris: Galilée.
—— (1992) *Jean Baudrillard: The Disappearance of Art and Politics*, W. Stearns and W. Chaloupka (eds.), New York: St. Martin's Press.
—— (1993) *Symbolic Exchange and Death*, Iain Hamilton Grant (trans.), London: Sage.
—— (1996) "Entrevue avec Jean Baudrillard," Graham Knight and Caroline Bayard (interview), *RSSI* 16 /1–2: 165–83.
Behar, Jack and Libermann, Ben (1968) "Paradise Regained or McLuhanacy?" in *The McLuhan Explosion: A Casebook on Marshall McLuhan and Understanding Media*, Harry H. Crosby and George R. Bond (eds.), New York: American Book Co.
Belfond, Jean-Daniel (1978–79) "Understanding Television," *Millésime* (June): 96–99.
Benoist, Jean-Marie (1968) "La nébuleuse McLuhan" (review), *La Quinzaine Littéraire* 43 (Jan. 15–31): 3–4.
—— (1978) *The Structural Revolution*, London: Weidenfeld & Nicolson.
Berger, René (1972) *La mutation des signes*, Paris: Denoël.
—— (1977) "L'enseignerie," *Diogène* 100: 87–111.
Bonnard, Laurent (1971) "McLuhan imposteur," *Le Tribune Lausanne* (April 10).
Bonnot, Gerard (1967) "Le prophète de télévision," *L'Express* (Sept. 25–Oct. 1): 83–86.
Borch-Jacobsen, Mikkel (1991) *Lacan: The Absolute Master*, Douglas Brick (trans.), Stanford: Stanford University Press.
Bourdieu, Pierre and Passeron, Jean-Claude (1963) "Sociologues des mythologies et mythologies de sociologues," *Les Temps Modernes* 211: 998–1021.
Bourdin, Alain (1970) *McLuhan: Communication, technologie et société*, Paris: Editions Universitaires.
—— (1978–79) "Un McLuhan dans le bibliothèque?" *Millésime* (June): 99–102.
Brecht, Bertolt (1979) "The Threepenny Opera," in *Collected Plays*, Vol. 2, Part 2, John Willett and Ralph Manheim (eds.), London: Eyre Methuen.
Brincourt, André (1972) "Si l'avenir donnait tort à McLuhan?" *Le Figaro* (July 15).
Burgelin, Olivier (1969) "Un essayiste pop: Marshall McLuhan," *Esprit* 382 (June): 1107–16.
Carpenter, Edmund (ed.) (1959) "Eskimo," *Explorations* 9.
—— (1966) "If Wittgenstein had been an Eskimo," *Explorations* [in *Varsity Graduate* 12/3 April]: 49–64.
—— and McLuhan, Marshall (eds.) (1960) *Explorations in Communication: An Anthology*, Boston: Beacon.

124

Cazeneuve, Jean (1969a) "Communications de masse et mutations culturelles," *Cahiers internationaux de sociologie* XLVI: 17–25.

—— (1969b) "MacLuhan est-il prophète?" *Les Nouvelles Littéraires* (July 31): 1, 7.

—— (1970) *Les pouvoirs de la télévision*, Paris: Gallimard.

—— (1972) *La société de l'ubiquité*, Paris: Denoël/Gonthier.

—— (1976) "MacLuhanisme," in *Les communications de masse: Guide alphabétique*, Paris: Denoël/Gonthier.

—— and Namer, G. (1969) "Sociologie de la connaissance: Les théories de MacLuhan" (review), *L'Année Sociologique* 20: 139–47.

Châtelet, François (1967) "Un nouveau faux prophète," *Le Nouvel Observateur* (Nov. 29–Dec. 5): 36–37.

Cox, Harvey (1967) "McLuhanite Christianity at Expo 67," *Commonweal* LXXXVI/10 (May 26): 277–78.

Csicsery-Ronay, Istvan (1988) "Cyberpunk and Neuromanticism," *Mississippi Review* 47–48: 266–76.

—— (1991) "The Sf of Theory: Baudrillard and Haraway," *Science Fiction Studies* 55: 387–404.

Curtis, James M. (1970) "The Function of Structuralism at the Present Time," *The Dialogist* II/2: 58–62.

—— (1972) "Marshall McLuhan and French Structuralism," *Boundary* 2 1/1: 134–46.

Debord, Guy (1990) *Comments on the Society of the Spectacle*, M. Imrie (trans.), London: Verso.

de Kerckhove, Derrick (1983) "Sources et prolongements de la pensée McLuhanienne," *Communication et langages* [Paris] 57: 55–65.

—— (1984) (ed.) *Pour comprendre 1984/Understanding 1984*. Communications présentées à l'occasion du colloque McLuhan et 1984. Centre culturel canadien, Paris, Dec. 14–16, 1983, Ottawa: Commission canadien pour l'UNESCO.

—— (1986) "Four Arguments for the Defence of Television," *Culture and Communications* [Budapest] 5: 43–65.

—— (1989) "Stratégies d'attention: la publicité télévisuelle en question," in *Le téléspectateur face à la publicité. L'oeil – l'oreille – le cerveau*, Collection Nathan-Université, Paris: Editions Nathan.

—— (1990) *La civilisation vidéo-chrétienne*, Paris: Retz.

—— (1991) *Brainframes: Technology, the Mind and Business*, Utrecht: Bosch & Keuning BSO.

—— and Sevette, Christian (eds.) (1990) *Les transinteractifs*, Actes du colloque, Nov. 4–5, 1988, Centre culturel canadien, Paris, Paris: ARTE.

Deleuze, Gilles and Guattari, Félix (1977) *Anti-Oedipus*, R. Hurley, M. Seem and H.R. Lane (trans.), New York: Viking.

Derrida, Jacques (1974) *Of Grammatology*, G. Spivak (trans.), Baltimore: The Johns Hopkins University Press.

—— (1982) "Signature Event Context," in *Margins of Philosophy*, Alan Bass (trans.), Chicago: The University of Chicago Press.

Desanti, Dominique (1974) "Marshall McLuhan, prophète de la communication – Il met en garde – 'Attention: le dialogue ou la mort'," *Argus de la Presse* (July 22): 40–41.

Dick, Philip K. (1964) *The Simulacra*, London: Methuen.

Dommergues, Pierre (1967) "La civilisation de la mosaïque – le message de Marshall McLuhan," *Le Monde* (Oct. 18).
—— (1969) "Marshall McLuhan en question," *Le Monde* (Aug. 9).
Dumur, Guy (1972) "La galaxie MacLuhan," *Le Nouvel Observateur* 401 (July 23): 36–37.
Emmanuel, Pierre (1969) "L'ère du système nerveux," *Les Nouvelles Littéraires* 2158 (Jan. 30): 1, 7.
Eno, Brian (1995) "Gossip is Philosophy," Kevin Kelly (interview), *Wired* (May): 146–51, 204ff.
Fekete, John (1973) "McLuhanacy: Counterrevolution in Cultural Theory," *Telos* 15: 72–123.
—— (1977) *The Critical Twilight: Explorations in the Ideology of Anglo-American Literary Theory from Eliot to McLuhan*, London: Routledge.
—— (1982) "Massage in the Mass Age: Remembering the McLuhan matrix," *Canadian Journal of Political and Social Theory* 6/3: 50–67.
Ferrier, Jean-Louis (1969) "Le scandale McLuhan," *L'Express* 912 (Dec. 30–Jan. 5): 45–46.
Finkelstein, Sidney (1968) *Sense and Non-sense of McLuhan*, New York: International Publishers.
Fischer, Hervé (1976) "Esthétique de mass média" in *Les communications de masse: Guide alphabétique*, Paris: Denoël/Gonthier.
Fischer, Hervé, Forest, Fred and Thenot, Jean-Paul (1975) *Collectif art sociologique: Théorie–pratique–critique*, Paris: Musée Galliera.
Fogel, Stan (1989–90) "Panic Compendiums," *Borderlines* 17: 40–42.
Frankovits, André (ed.) (1984) *Seduced and Abandoned: The Baudrillard Scene*, Glebe, NSW: Stonemoss Services.
Fulford, Robert (1971) "From Gurus We Always Get Enigmas," *The Toronto Star* (Sept. 25).
—— (1978) "Meet France's Marshall McLuhan," *The Toronto Star* (June 17).
Gane, Mike (1991a) *Baudrillard: From Critical to Fatal Theory*, London: Routledge.
—— (1991b) *Baudrillard's Bestiary: Baudrillard and Culture*, London: Routledge.
Gariépy, Renault (1967) "Etre ou ne pas être . . . McLuhanien! Mais comment l'être," *La Presse* (July 8).
Garric, Daniel (1967a) "Le prophète de l'information," *Science et Vie* 599 (Aug.): 24–9, 142, 144, 147.
—— (1967b) "La galaxie de Gutenberg de McLuhan," *Le Figaro* (Dec. 12).
Genosko, Gary (1994) *Baudrillard and Signs: Signification Ablaze*, London: Routledge.
—— (1998) *Undisciplined Theory*, London: Sage.
Gheerbrand, Gilles *et al.* (1969) *Pour comprendre M. McL.* Association des compagnons de Lure: Rencontres.
Giradin, Jean-Claude (1974) "Toward a Politics of Signs: Reading Baudrillard," David Pugh (trans.), *Telos* 20: 127–37.
Gould, Glenn (1984) "The Record of the Decade," in *The Glenn Gould Reader*, Tim Page (ed.), Toronto: Lester & Orpen Dennys.
Grigg, Russell (1991) "Signifier, Object, and the Transference," in *Lacan and the Subject of Language*, Ellie Ragland-Sullivan and Mark Dracher (eds.), London: Routledge.
Gritti, Jules (1972) "Un nouvel opium," *l'Arc* [Gutenberg issue] 50: 50–54.

REFERENCES

Guattari, Félix (1984) *Molecular Revolution: Psychiatry and Politics*, Rosemary Sheed (trans.), Harmondsworth, Middlesex: Penguin.

—— and Negri, Antonio (1990) *Communists Like Us*, Michael Ryan (trans.), New York: Semiotext(e).

Guissard, Lucien (1969) "Les intuitions de Marshall McLuhan," *Le Journal de la Croix* (Jan. 19–20): 7.

Hall, Stuart (1980) "Cultural Studies and the Centre: Some Problematics and Problems," in *Culture, Media, Language: Working Papers in Cultural Studies, 1972–79*, Stuart Hall, Dorothy Hobson, Andrew Lowe, Paul Willis (eds.), London: Unwin Hyman.

Heath, Stephen (1989) "Friday Night Books," in *A New History of French Literature*, Denis Hollier (trans.), Cambridge, Mass.: Harvard University Press.

Hoggart, Richard (1957) *The Uses of Literacy*, London: Chatto & Windus.

—— (1970) *La culture du pauvre: Etude sur le style de vie des classes populaires en Angleterre*, Paris: Minuit.

—— (1992) *An Imagined Life: Life and Times*, Vol. III (1959–91), London: Chatto & Windus.

Holland, Eugene (1988) "The Ideology of Lack in Lackanianism," in *Ethics/Aesthetics: Post-modern Positions*, Robert Merrill (ed.), Washington, DC: Maisonneuve Press, pp. 59–69.

Huyssen, Andreas (1989) "In the Shadow of McLuhan: Jean Baudrillard's Theory of Simulation," *Assemblage* 10: 7–17.

Ionesco, Eugène (1973) "MacBett," in *Plays*, Vol. IX, London: Calder & Boyars.

Jameson, Fredric (1983) "Postmodernism and Consumer Society," in *The Anti-Aesthetic*, Hal Foster (ed.), Seattle: Bay Press.

—— (1991) *Postmodernism, or The Cultural Logic of Late Capitalism*, Durham: Duke University Press.

Jarry, Alfred (1972) *Gestes et opinions du Docteur Faustroll*, in *Oeuvres complètes* I, Paris: Gallimard, pp. 657–732.

Kattan, Naïm (1965) "Marshall McLuhan, la comète intellectuelle du Canada," *Le Devoir* (Nov. 27).

—— (1967) "Marshall McLuhan" (review), *Critique* 238 (March): 322–34.

—— *et al.* (n.d. 1969[?]) *Análisis de Marshall McLuhan*, Alejandro Ferreiroa (ed.), Buenos Aires: Editorial Tempo Contemporaneo.

Kellner, Douglas (1987) "Baudrillard, Semiurgy and Death," *Theory, Culture & Society* 4/1: 125–46.

—— (1989) *Jean Baudrillard: From Marxism to Postmodernism and Beyond*, Stanford: Stanford University Press.

Knockaert, Yves (1988) *Third Interlude uit het ballet "MacLuhan at MacDonalds,"* Bruxelles: CeBeDem.

Kroker, Arthur (1980) "Capital of Hell," *Canadian Journal of Political and Social Theory* 4/1: 133–46.

—— (1981) "Life gainst History," *CJPST* 5/3: 93–8.

—— (1982a) "The Cultural Imagination and the National Question," *CJPST* 6/1–2: 5–11.

—— (1982b) "Augustine as the Founder of Modern Experience: The Legacy of Charles Norris Cochrane," *CJPST* 6/3: 78–119.

—— (1984) *Technology and the Canadian Mind: Innis/McLuhan/Grant*, Montréal: New World Perspectives.

—— (1985) "Baudrillard's Marx," *Theory, Culture & Society* 2/3: 69–83.

—— (1987) "Body Digest," *CJPST* 11/1–2: iii.

—— and Cook, David (1986) *The Postmodern Scene: Excremental Culture and Hyper-Aesthetics*, Montréal: New World Perspectives.

—— and Kroker, Marilouise and Cook, David (1989) *Panic Encyclopedia*, Montréal: New World Perspectives.

—— and Levin, Charles (1984) "Baudrillard's Challenge," *CJPST* 8/1–2: 5–16.

—— and Weinstein, M.A. (1994) *Data Trash*, Montréal: New World Perspectives.

Lacan, Jacques (1977a) *The Four Fundamental Concepts of Psycho-Analysis*, Alan Sheridan (trans.), London: The Hogarth Press.

—— (1977b) *Ecrits: A Selection*, Alan Sheridan (trans.), London: Routledge.

—— (1990) *Television*, Denis Hollier, Rosalind Krauss and Annette Michelson (trans.), Joan Copjec (ed.), New York: W.W. Norton.

Lambert, Gilles (1966) "Marshall McLuhan prédit la disparition des voitures," *Le Figaro Littéraire* 103 (March 3).

Languirand, Jean (1982) *De McLuhan à Pythagore*, Boucherville: Editions de Mortagne.

Lanoux, Armand (1967) "Les étranges idées de McLuhan," *L'Aurore* (Nov. 15).

—— (1968) "Un penseur op' art: MacLuhan," *Les Nouvelles Littéraires* 2140 (Sept. 28): 1.

—— (1973) "Introduction" to Marabini, Jean, *Marcuse & McLuhan et la nouvelle révolution mondiale*, Paris: Maison Mame.

Lévesque, René (1973) "La télévision: Le plus gros facteur révolutionnaire dans le domaine de la perception des gens, les uns par rapport aux autres," *Forces* 25: 13–23.

Levin, Charles (1984) "Baudrillard, Critical Theory and Psychoanalysis," *Canadian Journal of Political and Social Theory* 8/1–2: 35–53.

Lewis, Wyndham (1981a) "[Reprint of] *BLAST* 1" (June 1914), Santa Barbara: Black Sparrow Press.

—— (1981b) "[Reprint of] *BLAST* 2" (July 1915), Santa Barbara: Black Sparrow Press.

Lukács, Georg (1971) *History and Class Consciousness*, Rodney Livingston (trans.), Cambridge, Mass.: MIT Press.

Lyotard, Jean-François (1984) *Tombeau de l'intellectual et autres papiers*, Paris: Galilée.

—— (1993) *Libidinal Economy*, Iain Hamilton Grant (trans.), Bloomington: Indiana University Press.

Mandel, Ernest (1978) *Late Capitalism*, London: Verso.

Marabini, Jean (1973) *Marcuse & McLuhan et la nouvelle révolution mondiale*, Paris: Maison Mame.

Maras, Steven (1989) "Baudrillard and Deleuze: Re-viewing the Postmodern Scene," *Continuum* 2/2: 49–59.

Marchand, P. (1989) *Marshall McLuhan: The Medium and the Messenger*, Toronto: Random House.

Marcotte, Gilles (1974) "Marshall McLuhan et l'énergie du banal" (review), *Le Devoir* (June 15).

Mariet, François (1977) "Le macluhanisme dans l'éducation," *Le Français Aujourd'hui*
38 (June): 47–52.

—— (1978–79) "McLuhan, prophète ou imposteur?" *Millésime* (June): 107–9.

Marx, Karl (1936) *The Poverty of Philosophy*, New York: International Publishers.

Matson, Raymer B. (1968) "The Christian and McLuhan," *Dialog: A Journal of
Theology* 7: 259–65.

Mattelart, Armand and Stourdzé, Yves (1985) *Technology, Culture and Communications:
A Report to the French Minister of Research and Industry*, D. Buxton (trans.),
Amsterdam: Elsevier Science Publishers.

Mattelart, Michèle and Mattelart, Armand (1990) *The Carnival of Images: Brazilian
Television Fiction*, David Buxton (trans.), New York: Bergin & Garvey.

McLuhan, Marshall (1951) *The Mechanical Bride*, Boston: Beacon.

—— (1957) "The Liturgical Revival," *Explorations* 8 (October), no. 17 (n.p.).

—— (1962) *The Gutenberg Galaxy*, Toronto: University of Toronto Press.

—— (1964) *Understanding Media: The Extensions of Man*, New York: McGraw-
Hill.

—— (1966) "L'âge de l'électricité," Naïm Kattan (interview), *La Quinzaine Littéraire*
9 (July 15): 8–9.

—— (1967) *La galaxie Gutenberg: La genèse de l'homme typographique*, Jean Paré
(trans.), Montréal: Hurtubise HMH.

—— (1968a) *Pour comprendre les médias: Les prolongements technologique de l'homme*, Jean
Paré (trans.), Montréal: Hurtubise HMH.

—— (1968b) "Review of Pierre E. Trudeau, *Federalism and the French Canadians*,"
New York Times Book Review (Oct. 28).

—— (1968c) "Through the Vanishing Point," *The McLuhan Dew-Line Newsletter* 1/5
(Nov.).

—— (1969a) "The Mini-state and the Future of Organization," *The McLuhan
Dew-Line Newsletter* 1/8 (Feb.).

—— (1969b) "Strike the Set," *The McLuhan Dew-Line Newsletter* 1/11 (May).

—— (1969c) "Media and the Structured Society," *The McLuhan Dew-Line Newsletter*
2/1 (July).

—— (1969d) "Inflation as New Rim-Spin," *The McLuhan Dew-Line Newsletter* 2/2
(Sept.–Oct.).

—— (1969e) "Profiles of the 70's [Poster 6]," in "The End of Steel and/or Steal:
Corporate Criminality vs. Collective Responsibility," *The McLuhan Dew-Line
Newsletter* 2/3 (Nov.).

—— (1969f) *Mutations 1990*, François Chesneau (trans.), Paris: Maison Mame.

—— (1969g) "Marshall McLuhan," Eric Norden (interview), *Playboy* (March):
53–74, 178.

—— (1969h) "Vertical Suburbs and High-Rise Slums," *The McLuhan Dew-Line
Newsletter* 1/7 (Jan.).

—— (1970a) *Counterblast*, Harley Parker (design), London: rapp + whiting.

—— (1970b) "McLuhan on Russia: An Interview," Gary Kern (interview), *The
McLuhan Dew-Line Newsletter* 2/6 (May–June): n.p.

—— (1971a) "Marshall McLuhan: Révolution dans le village planétaire," Gerard
Moatti (interview), *Les Informations* [Paris] 137 (Sept. 29): 88–93.

—— (1971b) "MacLuhan," Roger Mauge (interview), *Paris Match* 1176 (Nov. 20):
14–17, 19, 22, 26.

—— (1971c) *Sharing the News: Friendly Teamness: Teeming Friendliness* (n.p.: McLuhan Associates and ABC).

—— (1972a) *Counterblast: Un ABC du McLuhanisme*, Jean Paré (trans.), Gilles Robert & Associés (adaptation de la maquette originale de Harley Parker), Montréal: Hurtubise HMH and Paris: Maison Mame.

—— (1972b) "Le passé-futur du livre," *Le Courier* (UNESCO) (Jan.): 16–20.

—— (1972c) "L'Express va plus loin avec Marshall McLuhan," *L'Express* 1075 (Feb. 14–20): 106–8, 116, 121–22.

—— (1973a) "Marshall McLuhan," Jean Paré (interview), *Forces* (Hydro-Québec) 22: 4–25.

—— (1973b) "McLuhan: Art et liberté," Derrick de Kerckhove (interview), *Vie des Arts* XVIII/72 (Autumn): 19–23.

—— (1974a) "Entretien avec Marshall McLuhan: Un mouvement invisible et spontané prend en charge la 'qualité de la vie'," Pierre Dommergues (interview), *Le Monde* (May 31).

—— (1974b) "MacLuhan parle de Giscard et des femmes," Pierre Martory (interview), *Paris Match* (June 15): 77.

—— (1975) "Fred Forest et le téléphone," in *Collectif art sociologique: Théorie–pratique–critique*, Hervé Fischer, Fred Forest, Jean-Paul Thenot (eds.), Paris: Musée Galliera.

—— (1976) "Pour une politique culturelle mondiale: un entretien avec McLuhan," Gilles Plazy and Odile Vande Walle (interview), *Les Nouvelles Littéraires* 2550 (Sept. 16): 2–3.

—— (1977a) *D'oeil à oreille*, Derrick de Kerckhove (trans.), Montréal: Hurtubise HMH.

—— (1977b) "Entretien avec Marshall McLuhan," Jacqueline Grapin (interview), *Le Monde* (Dec. 10).

—— (1979) "Avant-propos," in Sophie de Menthon, *Mieux utiliser le téléphone*, Paris: Les éditions d'organisation.

—— (1980a) "La galaxie 80," Jean Paré (adaptation), *L'Actualité* 5/1 (Jan.): 23–27.

—— (1980b) "Le vortex de Lewis: Art et politique en tant que masques du pouvoir," Emna Moalla (trans.), *Annales de l'Université de Savoie*: 47–51.

—— (1987) *The Letters of Marshall McLuhan*, selected and edited by Matie Molinaro, Corrine McLuhan and William Toye, Toronto: Oxford University Press.

—— (1995) *The Essential McLuhan*, E. McLuhan and F. Zingrone (eds.), Toronto: Anansi.

—— and Babin, Pierre (1977) *Autre homme, autre chrétien à l'âge électronique*, Lyon: Editions du Chalet.

—— and de Kerckhove, Derrick (1968) "Télévision et radiodiffusion 4: Mythologie et utopie," *Encyclopedia universalis*, vol. 15, Paris: Encyclopedia universalis France.

—— and Fiore, Quentin (1967) *The Medium Is the Massage: An Inventory of Effects*, New York: Bantam.

—— and Fiore, Quentin (1968a) *War and Peace in the Global Village*, New York: Bantam.

—— and Fiore, Q. (1968b) *Message et massage: Un inventoire des effets*, Thérèse Lauriol (trans.), Montréal: Hurtubise HMH and Paris: J.-J. Pauvert.

—— and Fiore, Q. (1970) *Guerre et paix dans le village planétaire*, Paris: R. Laffont and Montréal: Hurtubise HMH.

—— and Nevitt, Barrington (1972) *Take Today: The Executive as Dropout*, Toronto: Longman.

—— and Watson, Wilfred (1970) *From Cliché to Archetype*, New York: Viking.

—— and Watson, Wilfred (1973) *Du cliché à l'archétype. La foire du sens*. Accompagné du Dictionnaire des idées reçues de Gustave Flaubert, Derrick de Kerckhove (trans.), Montréal: Hurtubise HMH and Paris: Maison Mame.

Michel, Jacques (1972) "Marshall McLuhan: les jeunes Américains veulent être pauvres," *Le Monde* (July 16).

Miller, Jonathan (1971) *McLuhan*, Glasgow: Fontana/Collins.

Missika, Jean-Louis and Wolton, Dominique (1983) *La folle du logis*, Paris: Gallimard.

Monnier-Raball, Jacques (1979) *Simuler/dissimuler: Essai sur les simulacres de masse*, Paris: Payot.

Morin, Edgar (1968) *New Trends in the Study of Mass Communications*, Birmingham: Centre for Contemporary Cultural Studies, Occasional Paper No. 7.

—— (1969) "Pour comprendre McLuhan" (review), *La Quinzaine Littéraire* 69 (March 16–31): 16–18.

n[o].a[uthor]. (1967a) "Avec le maître," *Sept-jours* (July 15): 6–7.

n.a. (1967b) "Le professeur Marshall McLuhan estime que les Québécois sont des . . . hippies!" *La Presse* (Aug. 7).

n.a. (1970) "Guerre et paix dans le village planétaire" (review), *Le Monde* (Oct. 3).

n.a. (1973) "M. Jean Mistler oppose Gutenberg à McLuhan," *Le Monde* (Dec. 22).

Ory, P. (1991) "The Introduction of Science Fiction into France," in *France and the Mass Media*, Brian Rigby and Nicolas Hewitt (eds.), London: Macmillan.

Paik, Nam June (1986) "La Vie, Satellites, One Meeting – One Life," in *Video Culture*, John G. Hanhardt (ed.), Rochester: Visual Studies Workshop.

Paré, Jean (1968) "Qui est Marshall McLuhan?" and "McLuhan: son oeuvre et les enseignants," *L'Enseignement* [Journal de la corporation des enseignants du Québec] 5 (Nov. 15): 9–10, 11–12.

Pefanis, Julian (1991) *Heterology and the Postmodern: Bataille, Baudrillard, Lyotard*, Durham: Duke University Press.

Pétillon, Pierre-Yves (1969) "Avant et après McLuhan" (review), *Critique* 265 (June): 504–11.

Picard, Monique (1973) "L'homme revenu à l'âge des cavernes," *Tribune-Dimanche* (July 1): 5.

Picard, Raymond (1969) *New Criticism or New Fraud?*, F. Towne (trans.), Seattle: Washington State University Press.

Pontaut, Alain (1967a) "Tous les livres du monde dans une tête d'épingle," *La Presse* (July 8).

—— (1967b) "Du fond de cette galaxie," *La Presse* (July 8).

Rickels, Lawrence (1990) "Psychoanalysis and TV," *Substance* 61: 39–52.

Riesman, Paul (1966) "De l'homme typographique à l'homme électronique" (review), *Critique* 225 (Feb.): 172–82.

Rigby, Brian (1991) "The *Vivre son temps* Collection: Intellectuals, Modernity and Mass Culture," in *France and the Mass Media*, B. Rigby and N. Hewitt (eds.), London: Macmillan.

—— (1994) *"Popular Culture" in France and England: The French Translation of Richard Hoggart's "The Uses of Literacy"*. Monograph. Hull: The University of Hull Press.

Rosenthal, Raymond (ed.) (1968) *McLuhan: Pro & Con*, New York: Penguin.

Said, Edward (1971) "Abecedarium Culturae: Structuralism, Absence, Writing," *Triquarterly* 20: 33–71.

Sarick, Lila (1998) "Flash, Lingo Beat Fire, Brimstone," *The Globe & Mail* (April 11): A2.

Schaeffer, Pierre (1978–79) "Dialogue chaud et froid avec McLuhan," *Millésime* (June): 103–7.

Schafer, R. Murray, (1991) "The Theatre of Confluence I," *Descant* 73: 27–45.

Smart, Barry (1992) *Modern Conditions, Postmodern Controversies*, London: Routledge.

Starobinski, Jean (1979) *Words upon Words: The Anagrams of Ferdinand de Saussure*, Olivia Emmet (trans.), New Haven: Yale University Press.

Stearn, Gerald E. (ed.) (1967) *McLuhan: Hot & Cool*, New York: Dial Press.

Tassart, Maurice (1967) "Une bombe philosophique venue du Canada," *Carrefour* (July 19).

Texier, Jean C. (1968) "Un nouveau imposteur: Marshall McLuhan," *COMBA* (Aug.).

Theall, Donald (1971) *The Medium Is the Rearview Mirror: Understanding McLuhan*, Montréal and London: McGill-Queen's University Press.

—— (1973) "Les explorations esthétiques de McLuhan," *Vie des Arts* XVIII/72 (Automne): 14–18.

Thibau, Jacques (1970) *Une télévision pour tous les français*, Paris: Editions de Seuil.

Thomas, Bernard (1968) "H.M. MacLuhan: nous sortons de la galaxie Gutenberg pour entrer dans la galaxie Faraday," *Planète* 38 (Jan.–Feb.): 141–49.

Torgovnik, M. (1990) *Gone Primitive: Savage Intellects and Modern Lives*, Chicago: University of Chicago Press.

Turkle, Sherry (1981) *Psychoanalytic Politics: Jacques Lacan and Freud's French Revolution*, Cambridge, Mass.: MIT Press.

Vermillac, Michel (1993) *MacLuhan et la modernité*. Vols. I, II, Thèse de Doctorat Nouveau Régime de Philosophie, Epistémologie, Histoire des Idées. Présenté sous la Direction de Dominique Janicaud, UFR Lettres et Science Humaines, Université de Nice-Sophia Antipolis.

Vernay, Alain (1969) "La galaxie Gutenberg ou le prophète McLuhan," *Le Figaro* (Jan. 25).

Veyrac, Luc (1969) "McLuhan: ça sera pire," *Planète* (NS) 8 (June): 14–19.

Virilio, Paul (1986) *Speed and Politics*, Mark Polizzotti (trans.), New York: Semiotext(e).

—— (1989a) *War and Cinema*, Patrick Camiller (trans.), London: Verso.

—— (1989b) "The Last Vehicle," in *Looking Back on the End of the World*, New York: Semiotext(e).

—— (1992) "Une exposition très fin de siècle," *Le Monde* (April 16): 26.

Weinmann, Heinz (1977) "L'évangile selon Marshall McLuhan," *Le Devoir* (Dec. 24).

Wolf, Gary (1996) "The Wisdom of Saint Marshall, Holy Fool" and "The Medium is the Massage" and "Channeling McLuhan: The *Wired* Interview with *Wired*'s Patron Saint," *Wired* (Jan.): 122–31 and 182–87 *passim*.

Wolfe, Tom (1965) "What If He Is Right?" *New York Herald Tribune Magazine* (Nov. 21): 6–10, 22–24, 27–28.

Žižek, Slavoj (1991) *For They Know Not What They Do: Enjoyment as a Political Factor*, London: Verso.

REFERENCES

UNPUBLISHED ARCHIVAL MATERIAL

McLuhan Papers (*MP*), Social and Cultural Archives Program, National Archives of Canada, Ottawa, Finding Aid MG 31 D 156. The material is organized according to volume and file number.

MP 8/80. Naïm Kattan to McLuhan (Nov. 30, 1965).

MP 8/85. p.s. "McLuhan à la chaise électrique," *Partis Pris* (1966): 77.

MP 10/4. Gilles Anouil (editor-in-chief, *Réalités*, Paris) to McLuhan (Aug. 21, 1967).

MP 12/72. Misc. advertisement from *Le Monde*, May 8, 1974: 7.

MP 18/80. McLuhan to John Bassett (March 19, 1971).

MP 18/61. Pierre Babin to McLuhan (July 15, 1975).

McLuhan to Babin (Sept. 25, 1975).

Babin to McLuhan (Jan. 28, 1976).

Babin to McLuhan (Aug. 6, 1976).

McLuhan to Babin (March 13, 1978).

n.a., "Review of *Autre homme, autre chrétien à l'âge électronique*," *Centre for the Study of Communication and Culture Newsletter* [London] 1/2 (1979): 6–7.

MP 20/22. McLuhan to Cleanth Brooks (May 16, 1977).

MP 20/81. Claude Cartier-Bresson to McLuhan (July 13, 1973).

Cartier-Bresson to McLuhan (Sept. 21, 1973).

MP 22/17. McLuhan to Claude de Beauregard (Dec. 19, 1978).

MP 22/20. McLuhan to Mrs. Gertrude Le Moyne [*La Presse*] (Aug. 3, 1976).

MP 23/13. Jean Duvignaud to Cher Ami [McLuhan or de Kerckhove] (March 8, 1974).

MP 23/19. McLuhan to Tom and Dorothy Easterbrook (Aug. 1, 1972).

MP 38/30. Kenichi Takemura to McLuhan (Jan. 9, 1968).

K. Takemura to McLuhan (May 24, 1971).

K. Takemura to McLuhan (Sept. 27, 1973).

MP 134/31. McLuhan to François Hontis [*Le Monde diplomatique*] (April 30, 1970).

MP 137/1. Jean Sarrazin [Directeur, *Forces*, Hydro-Québec] to McLuhan (June 14, 1972).

MP 137/33. Typescript. McLuhan, "From Reporting to Programming: The Next One Hundred Years." French trans. D. de Kerckhove (1973).

MP 193/29. Marked manuscript by Roger Poole, "Embodiment and Text: A phenomenological inquiry into their relationship."

MP 193/30. Marked manuscript by R. Poole, typescript draft of a review of Derrida's *Of Grammatology*.

Shelagh Lindsey Collection, University of Manitoba Archives. Mss 20. Three boxes.

Box 2. Folder 1. *Telescope* (ms. transcript). Television interview with Marshall and family members. CBC Television, 1967.

NAME INDEX

SUBJECT INDEX